Jim,

Here's a tale from the great State of Mississippi that you might enjoy. The Pascagoula project was the start of our land conservation efforts in the Deep South.

Your friend,

Jim Mollison

Preserving the Pascagoula

by
DONALD G. SCHUELER

UNIVERSITY PRESS OF MISSISSIPPI
JACKSON
1980

To
Roxanna Sayre

This book has been published with the
cooperation and support of
The Mississippi Wildlife Heritage Committee

Library of Congress Cataloging in Publication Data
Schueler, Donald G.
  Preserving the Pascagoula.

  1. Nature conservation—Mississippi—Pascagoula
Swamp.   2. Pascagoula Swamp, Miss. I. Title.
QH76.5.M7S3   333.78'4   80-15931
ISBN 0-87805-123-6

Contents

Preface   vii

Introduction   xi

I   In the Beginning   3

II   Mississippi-As-It-Is   15

III   The Nature Conservancy   29

IV   The Heritage Program   50

V   The Wildlife Heritage Committee   60

VI   "Like A Pure Young Woman"   76

VII   In the Swamp   88

VIII   Quisenberry's Road Show   102

IX   The Legislative Battle   113

X   The Four Families   129

XI   Success   151

XII   The Future   164

Index   178

Preface

Land is the only thing in the world that amounts to anything, for 'tis the only thing in the world that lasts, and don't you be forgetting it. 'Tis the only thing worth working for, worth fighting for—worth dying for.

—Gerald O'Hara

THERE IS NOTHING new about telling Southerners the value of their land. O'Hara's words have been re-echoed from generation to generation. *Preserving the Pascagoula* is the fascinating story of how a disparate group of people worked and fought to preserve an immense tract of southern land, the magnificent Pascagoula Swamp, for the future benefit of the people of Mississippi. However, *Preserving the Pascagoula* is more than a suspenseful record of that achievement. The book is a blueprint of how a state government created from scratch the finest natural area program in America today.

I come from Boston, where we were always told that Mississippi was a backwards state. Backwards was a nice way of saying that Mississippi was full of ignorant redneck farmers, dissipated plantation owners, and corrupt cigar smoking politicians who spent all of their time harassing blacks and any "foreigner" who dared set foot in the state. This image was strongly reinforced by the media and Hollywood. It wasn't until I had become deeply involved with Mississippi and Mississippians that I realized how unfairly limiting that general impression was.

In 1974, when I first met the state's governor, Bill Waller, I sensed that he was somewhat on the defensive. While we were still shaking hands, he gave me a button that said "Rethink Mississippi." I am sure that a similar button was given to everyone the Governor met from north of Memphis. Since then, however, it has become obvious that many people are rethinking Mississippi. As Boston, Detroit, Newark and numerous communities demonstrate that racism is not restricted to the South, and as the quality of life in urban America continues to degenerate, Mississippi is coming into its own. Conservative estimates predict a 50% increase in Mississippi's population by the year 2000. Most people feel it will be much higher because the stigma that has protected Mississippi's great natural resources for so long is starting to wear off. Industry and individuals are asking themselves where else in America can they find a state that still has its great rivers, access to the Gulf of Mexico, a delta that can feed half the free world, a high yearly rainfall, a gentle climate and plenty of open land. In terms of renewable natural resources, I maintain that Mississippi is one of the richest states in America. This great wealth represents Mississippi's inheritance and now the time has come when the State must make critical decisions on how these resources are to be used.

The American frontier closed in 1890. Since then, America has been living on a fixed inheritance. But like irresponsible heirs, we have been spending our inheritance as if there were no tomorrow. From Beverly Hills to Fifth Avenue, success has been measured not by how much we save but by how much we consume. Conspicuous consumption is not recognized as the disease of waste but rather, the cure for an ailing economy. Now, we are starting to feel the crunch. The northeastern megalopolis, the Great Lakes industrial belt and the southern California freeway society are three examples of a degenerating life style. The people in these areas can no longer live in the irresponsible manner to which they have become accustomed. It is no wonder that people in these areas are starting to rethink Mississippi. It still has the natural resources they so very much need.

All of which puts Mississippi in a very enviable position. In the great growth race that has been going on since World War II, the state has always run last. But in the new race for untapped natural resources, Mississippi is without question right at the forefront, and apparently, it intends to stay there. Through its efforts to preserve the Pascagoula Hardwood lands, the State of Mississippi has begun to formally structure the latent respect and understanding that its people have always had for the land. This structure is called the Mississippi Natural Heritage Program, which is designed to identify and protect the State's most significant natural areas before they are destroyed.

It should be noted that this is not an environmental program in the traditional sense of the word. Its primary purpose is to help avoid conflict in a growing economy by providing objective and highly selective data to a wide variety of public and private decision makers so that the environmental confrontations which have held back economic growth in so many areas may be avoided. Whereas the environmental movement has its roots firmly planted in emotional conflicts, *the Mississippi Natural Heritage Program is based on the allocation of resources through the use of hard data.* Everyone, whether they represent industry, or environmental interests, has to have the facts before they can make rational decisions. Haphazard conservation is no better than haphazard development, because by arbitrarily stopping growth in one area, you arbitrarily force it into another. Mississippi is one of the few places in America that seems to realize this fact. That is why individuals and corporations have been able to join hands with government and make the Mississippi Natural Heritage Program more than just an idea. Through this growing partnership of individuals, corporations and government, all of them consulting the same objective data, significant natural areas within the state are being preserved.

It is a great misfortune that my home state did not have the same social responsibility when I was growing up. Instead of identifying and protecting the state's natural resources, the people of Massachusetts were content to consume everything in sight while they listened to the educators, politicians, and business leaders laugh at poor, ignorant Mississippi. Who's laughing now? The taxpayers of Massachusetts are being bled dry; the politicians are trying to avoid bankruptcy; the educators are re-evaluating plans for forced busing, and the business leaders are closing their factories and heading south.

All of which leads me to believe that America, the press, and even Hollywood would do well to rethink Mississippi. Forget the heat, forget the stereotypes, and focus on the blueprint that Mississippi has established for identifying, allocating and protecting its significant natural resources. *Preserving the Pascagoula* is that blueprint.

Dave Morine
Arlington, Virginia
March 20, 1980

Introduction

THIS BOOK HAS several purposes. The most obvious of them is to recreate one of the more exciting sagas in the history of wilderness preservation, the ultimately successful effort to protect the vast, little-known Pascagoula swamp in southeastern Mississippi. It is a story with several heroes, no great villians, and a happy ending. The environmental community, constantly beset by last-ditch battles, needs to be reminded now and then that the good guys sometimes win.

However, the victory itself is less significant in this case than the unusual strategy whereby it was achieved. From that tactical point of view, this is the story of the most effective nonprofit land acquisition group in the nation, the Nature Conservancy, and its innovative Natural Heritage Program which calls upon states to inventory and protect threatened wild species and ecosystems before they are assaulted by bulldozers and chain saws. It is also the story of one state's response to the heritage idea, which would serve as a model that other states could follow.

Finally, this is the account of a handful of dedicated people, ranging in their commitments from counterculture activism to staid conservatism, and in temperament from imaginative daring to stoic tenacity. Indeed, the actors in this environmentalist drama are so representative of the cross-currents of attitude and belief which characterized the early seventies that the mere fact that they could be reconciled with each other may be the most instructive part of this book. Their unlikely alliance suggests how much even a few individuals can accomplish, against great odds, if they have the will and the nerve.

Environmentalists often lament that their activism usually takes the form of reaction—of belatedly opposing the initiatives of developers only when yet another threatened species or wild area is on the verge of going under. The rescue of the Pascagoula Swamp could have been one more account of an eleventh hour confrontation. It is more than that because it suggests many ways in which people who want to save what is left of our wild heritage can instigate action themselves instead of waiting, as usually happens now, until the bulldozers are revving up to begin their work.

This book could not have been written without the assistance of many people connected with the Nature Conservancy, the Mississippi Wildlife Heritage Committee, and the Mississippi State Legislature, as well as various members of the "four families" who formerly held a controlling interest in the ownership of the Pascagoula Swamp. In particular, I would like to acknowledge my gratitude to Dave Morine, Avery Wood, Robert Hynson, Graham Wisner, and Bill Quisenberry for their invaluable help.

D. G. S.

Preserving the
Pascagoula

The Wildlife Heritage Committee acknowledges the technical assistance of Dr. P. T. Bankston, Director of the Governor's office of Science and Technology, and his staff who developed a preliminary assessment of the Pascagoula Heritage Project. This document was vital to the passage of the bill H.B. 914 of which these drawings were taken.

CHAPTER I

In The Beginning

IN THE FALL of 1973 two men who had little in common except their liking for each other met for lunch at a fashionable Washington, D.C. restaurant. One of the pair was Wayne Jackson, formerly an attorney and a high official in the Central Intelligence Agency, now retired. He was a small, frail-looking man, afflicted with many ailments including a chronic case of shingles that had badly scarred his face. He wore a dark conservative suit, and a fixed smile that was meant to conceal the continuous pain with which he lived. His companion was Graham Wisner, the youngest son of a distinguished Washington family who was now opposed to almost everything which that family—and Wayne Jackson, for that matter—represented. He was twenty-three, long-haired, dark-eyed, with finely made features that included a narrow patrician nose and a bowed mouth too small for his wide, thinly bearded jaw.

If a novelist wanted to create a character who embodied everything the counterculture of the late sixties and early seventies represented, he might begin by using Graham Wisner as a model. His rebelliousness was typical enough; like countless others of his generation he deplored his parents' lifestyle, the power structure and its representatives, and the governmental system which he regarded as amoral and militaristic. But not many others could claim, as Wisner was obliged to, that they had been born into the most privileged circles of the very establishment they condemned. The descendant of a wealthy southern family, Wisner had grown up in a Georgetown mansion where his mother regularly entertained many of the statesmen and politicians whom the radical movement most opposed. His father, now deceased, had been one of the creators of that *bete noir* of all radicals, the Central Intelligence Agency; during the fifties he had headed its Planning Division, better known to its critics as the Dirty Tricks Department. Even as a child, Graham had dimly understood that the senior Wisner dealt in matters like the Hungarian Revolution and the overthrow of the Guatemalan government much as other boys' fathers speculated on the stock market or sold cars. For the young man, opposing his parents and opposing the government were one and the same thing.

Graham's older brothers had found places for themselves in their parents' world without much difficulty. The oldest, Frank Jr., had joined the diplomatic corps, and the next in line, Ellis, after taking a Bachelor of Letters in philosophy at Oxford, had become manager of the family's business interests and a leading figure in Washington's cultural life. But for Graham Wisner and his sister, Wendy, the transition to equally respectable careers was checked by the events of the sixties. One cold winter day in 1965 when Graham was fifteen years old, his father, unable to struggle further against a worsening psychosis, chose to kill himself rather than become totally insane. Frank Wisner, Sr. had been an olympian figure in the eyes of his youngest son, wielding great, if vague, power—a man to whom other important people listened with respect. He had represented everything that seemed stable and unassailable in the nation's governing elite. Now his suicide had the shattering impact of an idol being overthrown. In its aftermath Graham began to correlate the stresses that had destroyed his father with those that were beginning to divide the nation and corrode the government from within.

By the time he was eighteen, Graham subscribed to most of the counterculture's politics of dissent. No actual break occurred between him and his mother and older brothers, the bonds of affection being too strong for that, but dinner conversation at the Georgetown mansion became a little strained. Wisner spent more and more time with his long-haired friends. For a year after leaving prep school, he lived in a

Washington ghetto, teaching at a black elementary school. Then, breaking with his family's preference for eastern Ivy League universities, he enrolled at Antioch, a college noted for its avant-garde curriculum and the antiestablishmentarian sentiment of its faculty and students.

During the years that followed, Wisner entered so wholeheartedly into the counterculture's lifestyle that his more orthodox relatives and friends wondered if he would ever emerge from it again. The restaurant meeting with Wayne Jackson in 1973 was a sort of answer. Jackson and Wisner had never altogether lost touch. Their relationship had begun in the latter's infancy when Jackson, a distinguished Washington attorney who worked for Frank Wisner at the CIA, became also his boss's confidante and a close family friend. At the time Jackson was a bachelor and a rather lonely man; it was natural that he should be regarded as an ex-officio favorite uncle in the Wisner household. Later he married and adopted two sons of his own, but his interest in his old friend's children continued. For their part, Graham, his sister, and his older brothers had looked to this firm, soft-spoken man as an independent source of adult understanding.

Now, despite a total contrast in political views, Graham continued to place a special value on his relationship with Jackson. At Antioch, obsessed with his father's role in CIA policies, Graham had researched the involvement of that now widely hated agency in the overthrow of the Guatemalan government. The project was in some sense an act of penance since he already knew that his father had masterminded the coup. Its chief beneficiary, as far as Graham could see, was the United Fruit Company, whose Guatemalan holdings had been in danger of being appropriated; its victims had been the country's duly elected officials and its people.

To this embittered view, Wayne Jackson offered some degree of balance. He had no sympathy with Graham's opinions but he had the good sense to treat the young man as a reasonably intelligent adult with a right to his own beliefs. While they dined, he carefully reconstructed— not for the first time—the international paranoia of the fifties: the deepening certainty in Washington that the Communist world was

intent on global domination, the escalation of the cold war, the fear that
some Latin American countries would follow Cuba into the Russian
camp, the consequent threat to America's security.

Jackson had no illusions that he would convince Graham that the
United States had been right in pursuing its "dirty tricks" policies. His
aim was to persuade the youth that, within the context of the times,
Frank Wisner, Sr. had done what he understood to be his duty at great
personal cost. Graham listened to these explanations with a new,
almost sympathetic, attention. By the fall of 1973 he had begun to
perceive that he was the creature of his own age as surely as his father
had been of his; and that that age—a mere decade more or less—was
coming to an end. The Vietnam war was winding down, the blue-collar
youths who recently had been beating up Graham's friends were now
wearing their hair long, and the black militants seemed more intent on
denouncing white liberals than white racists. Like others of his age and
class, he guessed that he might soon be stranded, still in his early
twenties, by the changing times—just as his father had been. Graham
Wisner wanted to make peace with the dead man's memory.

He was also touched by Wayne Jacksons loyalty in defending his old
friend. It occurred to him that during this reunion all the talk had thus
far been for his benefit. He hadn't even asked his one-time mentor how
he was getting along, although it was obvious that Jackson had aged
greatly in the last few years. He rectified this omission now. But the
older man avoided the subject of his failing health. Instead, somewhat
shyly, he confessed that he was writing a book.

It was about land easements, he said. When Graham looked mystified, Jackson explained that he was devoting his retirement to environmental issues, particularly the legal problems of acquiring conservation
easements on rural lands that were threatened by suburban and industrial development. This was a side of Jackson that young Wisner had
not known about; he was surprised and impressed. Enthusiastically he
began a discourse about his own interest in environmental issues. At
first, Jackson's thin smile became more fixed than usual. He expected
the youth's views on saving the environment to echo the countercul-

ture's party-line, which he regarded as long on rhetoric, short on specific solutions. But then Graham Wisner began to tell him about the Pascagoula Swamp.

By way of background, Graham explained that in 1970 he had become interested in film making. Under the free-for-all work-study program at Antioch, he was able to take off for Mississippi where he planned to produce a documentary about the lives of the men who worked the coastal oil rigs. He was in a fortunate position to study the subject since members of his extended family, headquartered in Laurel, Mississippi, directed Central Oil Company, in which his immediate family (the Wisners) had a substantial interest. Graham's father, having opted for a career in Washington, had voluntarily exiled himself from most of the family clan that still ruled in Laurel, but he had not relinquished his economic ties with them in spite of some disagreements about how their mutual business affairs were managed.

Graham had returned to the scene of his father's boyhood almost as a stranger. For a time he stayed with his recently widowed aunt, Mrs. Elizabeth Chisholm, in her large, oak-shaded home on Laurel's handsomest residential street, Fifth Avenue. Mrs. Chisholm had been a woman of advanced social views in the Mississippi of her own generation—too advanced in the opinion of many of her contemporaries. Among other philanthropic ventures, she had funded the college educations of several young black students, and she had recently earned some fame in the world at large by sponsoring the early career of Leontyne Price. Nevertheless she had as little in common with her long-haired nephew as other members of the Laurel clan. Graham's radical political views were unwelcome in Mississippi. He would not go to church; and his oil-smeared jeans (he was working as a roughneck on a rig to get material for his film) did not go well with his aunt's expensively upholstered sofas.

Before long, Graham moved to New Orleans where he lived for a year. There he involved himself in civil rights causes, fell in love, and lived the conventionally unconventional life that thousands of other affluent and alienated young people were living at the time. However, in one important respect Graham Wisner's experience was different. During his stay in Laurel, he had been reminded that one of the shared assets of the Wisners and their Laurel relatives was the Pascagoula Hardwood Company, which owned 42,000 acres of semiwilderness in southeastern Mississippi, consisting of cypress-tupelo swamps, oxbow lakes, bottomland forests, and pine ridges along the Pascagoula River. On the western shore of the river, in the middle of the tract, the family also owned a summer camp, long abandoned, where Graham was invited to stay whenever he liked. It was a large frame structure with a high roof and screened porches enclosing one enormous room. Long before, when his aunt and her contemporaries were young, the camp had been used as the base for family picnics, bridge parties, and fishing expeditions. Now it was in a state of disrepair. Leaves choked the rusting gutters and wasps' nests lined the rafters. The river current had eaten away most of the front yard and would soon undermine the house itself.

Once Graham had discovered this retreat, he began to visit it almost every weekend. Occasionally he brought a girl with him or a few of his "hippie" friends, but usually his only companion was a small white mongrel he had rescued from a New Orleans street. These interludes in his otherwise erratic life were a revelation of peace and simplicity. Since his boyhood summers at the Wisner farm on Maryland's eastern shore, he had retained a vague, inexpert affinity for the natural world, but this was the first time that he had ever experienced it as a presence that dominated his own. On some occasions he simply loafed on the porches of the camp or strolled in the nearby woods. Other times he slipped into the river, the mutt following him, allowing the current to carry him a mile or two downstream. Then, barefoot and half naked, he hiked back along the shore. During these expeditions he reacted with thrilled, amateur fear to the numerous cottonmouths basking peacefully on snags along the banks. At night he unrolled his sleeping bag in the single empty room, read *Tom Jones* or *Tropic of Capricorn*, or listened to the serenade of frogs outside.

Directly across the river stood a plain, durable frame dwelling, a typical southern "homeplace" raised on brick pilings. This was the home of Herman Murrah and his family, one of the few permanent dwellings in the Pascagoula Swamp. Murrah was a state game warden, but he also moonlighted as caretaker for the Pascagoula Hardwood Company. At one time his father had owned property on the river and operated a small cable ferry between his house and Graham's retreat. Murrah had tried on several occasions to persuade Pascagoula Hardwood to sell him the property on which the house stood, but so far the company had put him off.

Herman Murrah was a small, wiry man in his late thirties, with crow's feet at the corners of his eyes, a ready smile, and black hair that was almost gone on top. He had lived in the swamp all his life and probably knew it better than any other man alive. During high water years, the Pascagoula's waters sometimes flowed through his house. "Why hell," he would say, "when a flood came, we'd just pile up the furniture, open the front and back doors to relieve the pressure, and sit around the kitchen table eatin' fried squirrel. When the water started goin' down, we'd hop-to with brooms and sweep the mud out with the water. It was no big thing."

After a few weekends of observing the youth on the opposite bank skinny-dipping and otherwise making himself at home, Murrah decided to investigate. He crossed the river in his motorboat and introduced himself. What he thought of that first encounter with Wisner, apart from registering the fact that the young hippie was a part-owner of the property, is not recorded. But for Graham, the meeting was delight at first sight. Like most relatively sophisticated people with democratic aspirations, he had a genuine admiration for that rare American phenomenon, the uncommon common man. Which Murrah was, and knew it. The lively, sharp-witted swamper understood that he was an anachronism, tucked away in this isolated spot with owls and wildcats for neighbors; capable, if he had to, of living on the swamp's bounty. He liked being a colorful character. He had traveled widely within a narrow range, was a gifted raconteur, and, in spite of various hardships, seemed

to enjoy his life more than Graham did his. Before long he was regaling
Wisner with a string of anecdotes: about the morning he almost tripped
over a big cottonmouth on his doorstep; the night a farmer had stalked
him, thinking he was a poacher, while he stalked the real poacher; the
earlier times when he was a poacher himself, electrocuting fish, jack-
lighting alligators, shooting turkeys before dawn.

On subsequent weekends, Graham and his dog often swam across
the Pascagoula, a hundred yards in a strong current, to visit Murrah
and his family, occasionally staying for a dinner of fried catfish or
chicken. Several times he borrowed Murrah's small pea green boat and
took off into the swamp on his own. These hours alone, drifting
through the flooded forest, were the best times of all. He could not tell a
cypress tree from a tupelo gum, or a great blue heron from a little green
one; he had no idea that this becalmed grey-green land and waterscape
contained a remarkable collection of rare plant and animal species, or
that it was one of the last great riverine swamps remaining on the
continent. He would have liked it as well if there had been a hundred
others just like it. What impressed him was the obvious—the shadowy,
dusty stillness of the water, the fluted elegance of the trees, the unexpected whiteness of the sandy beaches, the sudden ascent of an egret. He
could imagine that he had drifted into a prehistoric present where
yesterday and tomorrow did not count. The plop of a disturbed turtle,
the cry of a hawk, the rustle of a skink in the mouldering leaves could
have been heard just now, or a thousand years ago. For a while he was
as free of himself as he was ever likely to be.

It was different, however, in the evenings when he and the dog were
curled in his sleeping bag, and the river current purred outside. He
would marvel that here in this unfamiliar wilderness which his family
owned but no longer visited, he had more the sense of coming home
than he had ever had in Laurel. Since he owned 1 percent of Pascagoula
Hardwood stock himself, he pretended that an equivalent part of the
property was personally his; he imagined what it would be like to claim
those 420 acres as a place where his independent, adult life could begin.

One of the first things he would do would be to sell Herman Murrah the couple of acres he wanted . . .

Unfortunately, he realized, owning shares in the Pascagoula Hardwood Company was not the same as owning the land that the shares represented. The company's director was Bob Hynson, a widower who had been married to his father's cousin. Graham had gotten along better with him than with some other members of the Laurel clan; they had even played tennis together once or twice during the weeks he lived with his aunt. But he had no luck petitioning him on Murrah's behalf. Hynson had listened to him sympathetically, and then explained that the swamp would probably be sold to a larger timber company before too long; therefore it would not do to cut small parcels out of the middle of it that would depreciate its value like holes in a blanket.

Not long after this, Hynson and the other officers of Pascagoula Hardwood would modify this view enough to make an exception of Murrah, selling him the small plot he desired; but Graham couldn't know this at the time. Besides, he was not disposed to give the Laurel families the benefit of any doubt. All he could think of was the discrepancy between Murrah's personal attachment to the swamp, his wish to stake a small claim to it, and his own family's absentee landlordliness which regarded the Pascagoula solely as a financial holding. His sympathy for Murrah's plight was intensified because he felt that his own position was not dissimilar. Of the four related families that controlled most of Pascagoula Hardwood's stock, the Wisners, including Graham, owned the least—8 percent— and therefore had little say about its fate. There had already been considerable disagreement among the families about what that fate should be. Compared with other shared investments, especially the Central Oil Company, Pascagoula Hardwood was a small operation; and Graham was not the only one who felt that its officers were too preoccupied with their other business ventures to give it much attention. Certainly it had not returned any dividends in years. The considerable number of nonfamily shareholders who owned very small amounts of stock were, generally, eager to sell the property at once. Hynson and the company's vice-president, Gardiner Green, were among those who were in no hurry. They argued that with every year the maturing timber increased in value and the property appreciated. If a sale were concluded, it should be at terms that would not leave the larger stockholders vulnerable to heavy federal and state taxes. There were also a few shareholders—notably Graham's older brother, Ellis— who toyed with the idea of intensively managing the land as a family business. These last were in the minority, however. The likelihood was that the families would sell when the terms were right. When that happened, the swamp would quite possibly be clear-cut and would cease to exist as Graham had known it.

Graham imagined what it would be like if he had the final say. For all his vaguely socialist inclinations, he could easily see himself as the benign ruler of this watery fief. It would not be a bad thing to return to the Mississippi of his origins, now that the New South was on its way, to reclaim some part of that inheritance which his father had left behind. His side of the family were agreed that if the senior Wisner had stayed in Mississippi he would have had much influence on the clan's fortunes, and they would all be even wealthier than they were. In Graham's case, however, these speculations had a selfless motive. The Pascagoula was the only part of his inheritance that he valued for itself, and his overriding wish was to save it. It did not occur to him that it could be preserved in a pristine condition. He took it for granted that preservation meant altruism, outright donations; and although the Wisners and their Laurel connections had their philanthropic enthusiasms, the Pascagoula was not one of them. As Bob Hynson had explained, the interests of the stockholders had to come first. The only possible solution that Graham could see was to make Pascagoula Hardwood an active and profitable company, managing the timber resources of the swamp on a sustained yield basis, rather than leveling the entire forest. That way, only relatively small acreages would be clear-cut and replanted at a time. The swamp would be less wild and beautiful than he had found it, but at least it would survive. But, when Graham discussed this idea with Hynson, it became clear that the latter regarded the eventual sale of the property as inevitable.

Early in 1971, Graham left the South to return to Antioch. For a while he continued to be active in the great causes of the hour. During the Cambodian invasion he returned to Washington to join thousands of other students in demonstrations to be held there. It was indicative of his privileged position, even as a rebel, that he could meet Henry Kissinger under his mother's roof and tell him that, next day, he would be marching "against your war." However, Kissinger had laughed indulgently and turned away.

During the next two years, the opportunities for confrontation swiftly diminished. Already many adherents of the counterculture were listening to, if not yet following, different drummers. Graham was reasonably happy at Antioch, but as time went on he increasingly remembered the weekends spent in the Pascagoula as a short-lived golden age. The swamp remained the one unchanging presence in his changeful life.

In the summer of 1973, he learned that Masonite Corporation, one of the largest timber companies in the world, had made a bid to acquire Pascagoula Hardwood Company through a tax-free exchange of stock, and that it would probably be only a matter of time before the clear-cutting began. Desperately, Graham contacted the Audubon Society, the only large conservation organization he knew anything about. When he explained as much as he knew of the circumstances of the impending sale, he was told that there was nothing the Society could do.

This was where matters stood in the fall of 1973, when Wayne Jackson happened to mention his own environmental interests to his young friend, and Graham, eager for advice, recounted everything he knew about the Pascagoula and his family's connection with it. Jackson listened thoughtfully. When he finally spoke, it was to ask Graham if he had ever heard of an outfit called the Nature Conservancy. Graham shook his head. Jackson explained that he had been doing much of his research on easements at the Conservancy's headquarters in Arlington, Va. and was familiar with the way the organization worked. It was unique among private environmental groups in that it devoted its activities solely to land acquisition. It had saved a great many important natural areas, sometimes snatching them out from under a developer's nose. Although most of these properties were acquired through donations, the organization could put up hard cash for land when it had to, often reselling it later to a state or federal agency.

Graham's face brightened. "Do you think—"

"Don't get your hopes up," Jackson warned him. "From what you've been telling me, I doubt that even the Conservancy can help you."

"But would you tell them about it anyway? Even if there's only a small chance?"

Jackson smiled. This was the first time in a long time that any of his old friend's children had asked his help for anything. "Well," he said, "there's no harm in asking, is there?"

CHAPTER II

Mississippi-As-It-Is

BY THE AUTUMN OF 1973, the old Robert E. Lee Building, one of the first skyscrapers in Jackson, Mississippi, had lost its original identity as a hotel, yielding to the more modern Holiday Inn across the street. Instead of being torn down, however, it was being converted into an office building occupied by various state agencies, among them the state Game and Fish Commission. Not all the interior alterations were completed. The third-floor office of the then director of the commission, Avery Wood, was a large corner room, twice its present size. Even so, it could barely contain its energetic occupant on this November afternoon.

Wood was alone at the moment; he had just ended a conference, one of a long series, with his advisors, Bill Quisenberry, a member of the commission's staff, and Bruce Garretty, a state attorney assigned to the commission as legal counselor. Their discussion had left Wood even more agitated than he usually was. He pulled away from his desk and paced to the window, staring out over the intervening parking lots at the impressive dome of the state capitol; then, after a moment or two, he prowled back across the room to a large portable blackboard stationed near the door. On the wall next to it was a sign which stated GREAT MINDS DISCUSS IDEAS . . . AVERAGE MINDS DISCUSS EVENTS . . . SMALL MINDS DISCUSS PEOPLE.

For some time Wood glared at the tangle of numbers and illegible abbreviations chalked on the blackboard's surface, all the while puffing

15

his cigarette and absentmindedly tapping his upper lip, checking for the moustache that wasn't there. He missed his moustache. The governor had asked him to shave it off because so many people had complained that he looked hippie enough even without it. Actually, with his shaggy, prematurely gray hair, wrinkled shirt, and steel-rimmed glasses, Avery Wood looked more like an eccentric physics professor than an overaged flower child. But he had obliged the governor. Given the realities of political life, it was remarkable, even admirable, that the moustache was the only thing Bill Waller had ever asked him to compromise about.

Just now, however, it was not compromise but money—the lack of it—that was on Avery Wood's mind. By rights he should have been a happy man, at least professionally; and in some sense he was. Other people might only daydream about what they would most like to be—a rock singer, president of the United States, a billionaire. But Avery Wood had wanted to be director of the Mississippi Game and Fish Commission more than anything else in the world, and now, without any special qualifications, that was what he was. His was a political appointment, his reward for supporting Waller both in his unsuccessful gubernatorial campaign in 1967 and the winning one in 1971. Although Wood had no money to contribute, he had believed in Waller and worked hard to round up votes for him. For his part, Waller liked and trusted Wood. Both men were strong-willed, impulsive, and "country." In the relatively cosmopolitan atmosphere of Jackson, Waller liked to have people around him with whom he felt at home.

"When Bill Waller got elected," Wood recalls, "he said to me, 'Avery, I'll give you any reasonable appointment you want because I know you'll do the best you can. Just don't catch any flak.' Well, I don't know about the flak, but I sure as hell meant to do my best. I didn't have any technical knowledge of wildlife management but I loved hunting and fishing and wildlife and all that, and I knew something had to be done or we weren't going to have those things like we used to. To tell the truth, I never did have a whole lot of kind things to say about the people who were running the Game and Fish Commission at the time. It looked like they were using it as a play-toy for a select group of people.

The average sportsman was absolutely excommunicated from an input point of view. No one was looking down the line to where average people, poor people, could hunt and fish in a hundred years. And now here was the governor telling me I could direct the commission! All of a sudden I'm not on the outside anymore with my nose against the glass, complaining about what 'they' aren't doing right. I'm them! I got to put up or shut up."

In November, 1973, Avery Wood had been on the inside, looking out, for about fifteen months. All things considered, he had done fairly well. He had managed to convince the state legislature to support a needed increase in fishing and hunting license fees, and he had tried, though with only limited success, to discover a few people in the department who weren't, as he puts it, "shell-shocked" from years of bureaucratic and political fence-walking. But Wood was still a long way from the promise he had made himself on the day his appointment was announced.

The occasion was one that he still vividly remembers. He was in a joyful frame of mind, his wild, amateur's dream a signed and sealed reality. There he was in the governor's office, lined up with the commissioners who had been appointed with him, being introduced by Waller to the press and TV newsmen. Big smiles and warm words circulated freely; there was a pat on the back from the governor; television cameras whirred; old duck hunting buddies from his native Greenwood applauded loudly. A heady moment. Then, after the introductions were finished, the conference was opened to questions from the newsmen.

There was no build-up to what followed. The first question from a reporter hit Avery like a blow in the face: "Mr. Wood, have you ever been arrested for a game law violation?"

Wood is still convinced that the question had to be planted by someone who had served in the Game and Fish Commission under the previous administration. "That's the only way the reporters could have got that information. There's no way it could have been just a shot in the dark. Anyway, there was nothing to do but tell the man, yes, I'd been arrested, but the case was dismissed. It was an uncomfortable moment, you can believe that. Here I am, not even out of the shower yet, not even in my office. . . ." He winces, thinking of it. "I felt worst of all for the governor. He was trying to put a good face on it, but there was a lot of people who thought Waller was a country bumpkin, you know? And that the people surrounding him were country bumpkins too who wouldn't even know where the men's room was. And so here was Waller, honest as hell, introducing a damn game law violator as his new game and fish director. I mean, I felt bad!"

Wood admits that when he was a youth out duck hunting with his lifelong friend, Bill Barrett, the two of them, and everyone else they knew, took more than the legal limit. "Back then we didn't think there was any way in the world you could shoot too many ducks, there was so many of them." Ironically, that *laissez faire* attitude had long vanished by the fall of 1971 when Wood was charged for the first time with a violation. The circumstances were simple enough: the law required that a gun used in duck hunting must be "plugged" so that it can hold only three shells at a time. Wood had lost the plug in his own gun so he borrowed one of Barrett's shotguns. Since Barrett was positive that it was plugged, Wood didn't check it. Soon after, they were in a blind on a Delta lake. No ducks showed up, but a game warden did; and a minute later Avery Wood was holding a citation for hunting ducks with an unplugged gun.

The following day, during his lunch break, he drove up to Slaughter, Mississippi, to pay the fine. When he arrived at the judge's office in the little town, a number of local farmers and businessmen had gathered at the cotton gin outside. Word had gotten around that "they done captured Avery." "I wanted this thing to go down right," Wood explains, "so I told the judge, 'Bubba, I'll pay the fine.'" However, by this time Waller had won the governor's race in the Democratic primary and it was well known in the Delta country that his supporter, Avery Wood, might soon be riding high on Fortune's wheel. The judge informed Avery that he wanted to talk to him privately in his office— where, as it turned out, Avery didn't have to say a word. "The judge told me he knew I wouldn't shoot with no unplugged gun, which was true.

All the same, I tried to pay that fine. But he told me to go on. And that was the last I heard of it 'til July, '72, when the reporter asked that question in the governor's office."

As matters turned out, the media let Wood off. Since he had not been convicted, the incident was not publicized. But Wood did not know this when he left the state capitol and dejectedly walked the few blocks to his new office. He had been in the building only once before, when it was still the Robert E. Lee Hotel and he was an adolescent playing football for Greenwood High School. The Greenwood team had been billeted at the hotel while they were in Jackson to play against their arch rival, Jackson Central High. Avery's team lost, and the grown man still recalls how depressed his boy self was when he returned to his room following the game. Now, two decades later, he was entering the same building after taking a beating once again. With a characteristic flair for melodrama, he rechristened the place the Heartbreak Hotel. As soon as he reached his new office and closed the door behind him, he announced to the unfamiliar, not-yet-cluttered room, "I'm going to do this job better than anybody has before. I'm going to do something really important. Give me some time and I'm going to turn this place around!"

That had been sixteen months ago. Now there was no longer any doubt in Avery Wood's mind about the really important something he had to do. The trouble was that he couldn't figure out how to do it.

Myopically, he peered at the scrawled figures on his blackboard although he already knew them by heart. They were informing him that since 1965—less than a decade—nearly a million new acres in Mississippi had been converted into cropland. A quarter million more had gone into pasture. Tens of thousands of additional acres had been cleared for subdivisions, industrial expansion, highways. Most of Mississippi's hardwood bottomland forests had vanished for good. During the same period, 2,500 miles of the state's rivers and streams had been destroyed by channelization. These developments were accompanied by a rise in the state's population, and according to current projections there would be a further increase of almost 50 percent within the next generation.

The hieroglyphic data on the blackboard had been painstakingly researched by Wood's aide, Bill Quisenberry. Ungratefully, Wood gassed it with cloud after cloud of exhaled smoke. He realized that most Mississippians, beginning with his boss, the governor, would cheerfully regard the figures as evidence of the state's economic progress—which, if anything, only intensified his own gloomy view of them.

The swiftness with which Mississippi's streams and forests were disappearing dismayed Avery Wood, but Quisenberry's data had not come as a complete surprise. In a local way, he had already experienced what those facts and figures were telling him. When he was a boy growing up in the Delta country, he and his father, and his friend, Bill Barrett, had always had their pick of places to hunt and fish in the area around Greenwood. There were any number of favorite spots, one that was best for squirrels, another for deer, others for ducks; and there were a hundred places to fish without seeing anyone else all day. But when Wood returned from the Navy in 1956 he discovered that much had changed. "Hell," he exclaims, "when I got back there were places I'd hunted squirrels where the very trees were gone. All sorts of areas that had been open to us as kids were posted or cleared off entirely. It seemed like it was happening overnight."

Wood was witnessing the side effects of an agricultural revolution. The vast Delta plain of western Mississippi, recharged for centuries by the alluvial soil deposited whenever the Mississippi River and its tributaries overflowed their banks, was the most favored agricultural land in the state. It was also exceedingly rich in wildlife. During the years of Wood's young manhood, the region experienced great change. For one thing, soybeans were competing with cotton as the chief money crop of the area. For another, a new agricultural technology was not only displacing manpower but requiring farmers to enlarge their holdings in order to make their capital investment in huge new farm machines worthwhile. Soon the traditional farm and plantation system was all but gone; agribusiness, of the type already established in the Midwest, had become the rule.

During the same period—the fifties and sixties—the region's 4 million acres of bottomland forests were rapidly drained in a series of projects—many of them frankly "pork-barrel"—promoted by the U.S. Corps of Engineers and the Soil Conservation Service. Thus made vulnerable, virtually all of these hardwood forests, the Big Woods of Faulkner's hunting stories, were bulldozed away in a handful of years, to be replaced by mile after mile of open fields. The rural poor, made expendable by technology, emigrated to Detroit and Chicago where they were soon doing some displacing of their own. The black bear and the ivorybill, with nowhere to go, vanished.

As Wood would later learn, the agricultural revolution which he was witnessing had its silvacultural counterpart in the hilly, less fertile lands east and south of the Delta. The ubiquitous pine was no longer a tree but a crop to be planted, weeded, genetically improved, and harvested like any other. The vast woodlands owned by the U.S. government and the timber industry, more than one-fourth of Mississippi's forested land area, had traditionally supported mixed stands of pines and hard- woods. Now tens of thousands of these acres were being bulldozed, disked, and planted to fast-growing slash pine seedlings, the upright rows often extending for miles, with now and then a creek or branch to break their regimental geometry. These even-growth plantations could be managed to reach marketable size in a remarkably short span of years and then harvested by clear-cutting. The result was increased profits for the timber industry and increased supplies of paper for the nation. However, the pine plantations created by the new technology were a wasteland from an ecological point of view, where few indige- nous species of animals, birds, or even plants survived except in the mercifully abundant run-off branches and gulleys where men and ma- chines bogged down.

The demographic, economic, and environmental changes imposed upon the landscape by these new conditions were so encompassing that it was difficult for Wood and his associates to assess their toll. Certainly quail, rabbits, and other upland game had declined along with the number of small farms. Squirrel and duck populations were also much reduced. Red wolves, and probably the panther, were gone, and the black bear nearly so. An undetermined number of nongame species, from eagles to cockaded woodpeckers, were disappearing unremarked. One of the few bright spots was the fact that the deer herd had continued to expand.

Discouraging as this tally was, Avery Wood was even more discouraged by the prospect that lay ahead. The past impact of technological change could almost be considered mild compared with the changes that were now underway. During the sixties, Mississippi's much publicized racial turmoil, and, later, the economic recession, had kept industrial development marking time. But all this was changing now. The counties around Jackson were already given over to light industry and expanding suburbs. On recent trips down to the Gulf Coast, Wood had seen for himself the unplanned growth of heavy industry, highways, tourism, in spite of the hammer blow that Hurricane Camille had dealt the area in 1969. Even now, as environmental regulations tightened in the Northeast, corporations were eyeing Mississippi's bays and inlets as prospective sites of new plants. The New South was obviously on its way. And the obvious "important thing" that Avery Wood had to do was to preserve as much of its unspoiled wilderness as he could while there was still time.

Wood is not sure how he comes by his activist temperament. "I ain't never had no bad childhood or any of that crap," he explains, "but I guess I could be described as an angry man. Anyways, a lukewarm hothead. I just think more people should get angry more of the time when things ain't being done right." He automatically sides with the underdog, giving what assistance he can to young people who get in trouble with their parents or the law. During the sixties his dislike of bullying led him to support civil rights for blacks. However, in a more general way his views are hardly extreme. He has no great liking for big government, especially big federal government, and his unrevolutionary concept of reform in state government is that politicians and bureaucrats should be more honest and hard-working, and do a better job of looking after the interest of "the little fellow." Wood favors programs that "make tax*payers* out of people, not tax burdens," and he believes that Mississippi's racial problems are essentially economic in origin. With views like these, he can hardly oppose the growth of industry in the state. "But what matters," he argues, "is where and how it grows."

Wood credits Ducks Unlimited, an international organization dedicated to halting the decline in migratory waterfowl populations, with making an active conservationist of him. "They were getting a chapter started in Greenwood in the early sixties," he remembers, "so me and my buddy Barrett went to the meeting. Here were these guys from Canada talking about the same things happening up there that were going on here. For the first time I began to understand the scope of the problem. It seemed to me that the course they were on, acquiring habitat for ducks, was what had to be done for all wildlife. That was when I started thinking of what I would do if I was director of Mississippi Game and Fish, not knowing then it was anything but a crazy dream."

Addicted as he is to hunting and fishing, Wood views the seemingly inevitable reduction in Mississippi's wildlife resources as more than a loss of recreational opportunities. He has difficulty articulating the connection but he is convinced that it would fundamentally alter the character of the state and its people. After the headlines of the sixties, many Americans might exclaim, "Good!" to such a prospect; and Mississippians themselves are uncomfortably aware that they are at the bottom of the heap, or close to it, in studies concerning income levels, educational quality, and the like. Nevertheless, most of them, including Wood, evidently share the view of Willie Martin, the senior secretary outside his office: "I know how everybody claims we're backward and all," she says, "so I guess I'm just backward too. Because I kind of like Mississippi the way it is."

In speaking of Mississippi-the-way-it-is, Mrs. Martin is not referring to pay scales or public services, which she would undoubtedly like to see improved. Her concern is for another aspect of the state's backwardness —the fact that it preserves, to a degree rare in modern America, a sense of community and a system of values that are shared by almost all its citizens. Despite the social and racial problems, Mississippians are culturally a homogeneous lot. The majority of them, black and white, belong to or derive from the countryside and the small county seats; they still subscribe to small town mores, country manners, and belief in a Protestant God. Even in Jackson's booming suburbs, most of the inhabitants are no more than a generation away from the rural counties.

To visitors from northern or West Coast cities, the atmosphere can be dismayingly intimate. Downtown Jackson is not yet Atlanta, and can be easily walked from one end to the other. Pedestrians stop what they are doing to give the stranger detailed directions, waitresses call their customers "honey," and young people address adults as "Sir" or "Ma'am." In Avery Wood's hometown, Greenwood, the cotton brokers meet twice a day at a Market Street Cafe where they exchange leisurely small talk and play a numbers game to see who buys the coffee. The Holiday Inn at the edge of town is almost a club where all the traveling salesmen know each other and the desk clerk greets each of them by his first name.

Kinship ties are strong, and everywhere there is an insular sense of place. State politicians live close to their constituents and stop to talk with them on the streets. The Establishment continues to send its sons and daughters to Ole Miss or Mississippi State, depending on which they went to themselves, even when they could afford to export them to more prestigious institutions out of state. And it is axiomatic that if two persons meet who live at opposite ends of Mississippi, there is a good chance that at least one of them will know people the other knows.

In short, Mississippi is an anachronism, a cultural remnant of a United States that for most Americans ceased to exist forty years ago. It retains most of the flaws associated with a provincial society, yet its citizens persist in being fond of it. And even the most hardened cosmopolite would probably admit the appeal of a social order in which alienation, anonymous violence, congestion, and the decay of family and neighborhood ties are still not the rule.

For Avery Wood, however, more than nostalgic sentiment was

involved; it was the state's present, not its past, that was in danger of being lost. As far as he was concerned, Mississippi-the-way-it-is had less to do with its antebellum nostalgia, its lost cause, or even its racial inequality, than with the abiding presence of its fields and forests, swamps and streams. Perhaps in no other state, not even the Far West or Alaska, were the lives and pastimes of ordinary citizens so wedded to the out-of-doors. Almost everyone seemed to hunt or fish. In a population of some 2 million people, over 600,000 hunters and fishermen bought licenses during Wood's first year in office. In the same year outdoor recreation generated about $150 million worth of business in Mississippi and contributed $7 million in unsolicited tax revenue to the state's general fund.

Wood was dutifully interested in the economic significance of these figures, but they were more important to him as evidence that hunting and fishing were the most cohesive and enduring expression of the Mississippian's way of life. Middle-aged people easily remembered how, during the depression, the free bounty of forests and streams literally helped to keep body and soul together. At that time the deer herd was almost gone from the state, but squirrels, rabbits, raccoons, opossums, ducks, quail, bream, bass, and, in the southern counties, the marine resources of the Gulf, were available in seemingly inexhaustible numbers, taking turns on the tables of otherwise destitute people.

Now, in economically better days, the collective memory of those hard times was much softened by individual recollections of afternoons on some obscure stream or cypress-shaded slough, or mornings in the dappled woods. In such settings, boyhood friendships like that between Avery Wood and Bill Barrett were confirmed for life, and adults like Wood's father got to know their sons. Avery Wood believed that if these traditional experiences were not still the best, most shared and sharing influence in the lives of Mississippians, it would be difficult to say what else was.

As director of the Game and Fish Commission, Wood was in a better position than most to know that there was a lot wrong with the tradition. The state had more than its share of game law violators, people who jacklighted deer just as their fathers had, who used non-game species as target practice, littered the woods, allowed their deer hounds to roam loose at all seasons, running down does and fawns. Or who shot more than their limit of ducks, as Wood had when he was a boy. But he had changed, and he wondered if that was not the point: paradoxically, Mississippians would have to learn to change in order to keep Mississippi-the-way-it-is.

Wood could console himself that at least there weren't yet great weekend hunter-armies of industrial workers invading the woods as they did up North. There were no game ranches like those in Texas, or target shooting of short-stopped flocks of ducks as at the midwestern refuges. And in Mississippi, hunting hadn't become technological warfare—with off-road vehicles, walkie-talkies, super scopes and the rest—not quite yet, anyway. For the moment, most hunting and fishing in the state was an exercise conducted in solitude or with a small group of friends. People went out with shotguns and dogs, or in a johnboat with rod and reel or a cane pole.

Staring at the figures on his blackboard, Wood was beset by a sense of urgency. The administration of which he was a part was frankly wooing northern industry with descriptions of the state's exploitable resources. Waller himself smiled from the advertising pages of national magazines, promising every conceivable tax exemption to out-of-state businesses in search of a new home. Wood realized that it would require political far-sightedness of an unprecedented kind to counterbalance that siren call to industry with a determination to control growth in the interest of Mississippi-as-it-is. Yet land zoning, or any other kind of regional land management, was anathema to the state's politicians. If hunting and fishing were to be maintained as part of Mississippi's inheritance, the only alternative was to initiate a land acquisition program, and soon.

At present, the Game and Fish Commission leased a number of tracts from the major timber companies, but in terms of long-range management these lands were of little value. There was no way that the timber industry's goal of raising the greatest possible number of pines per acre could coincide with the commission's need to raise the maximum populations of wildlife. Except for these lands and tracts leased on U.S. Forest Service lands, the only tracts that the commission had under its control were a paltry 21,000 acres that it had acquired with funds generated from the sale of hunting and fishing licenses. The legislature had never appropriated general fund monies for wildlife management lands. There were always other priorities; and in any case, few people in the state had the equivalent of Avery Wood's blackboard staring them in the face.

As a result of his discussions with Quisenberry and commission attorney Bruce Garretty, Wood had begun to take some action. Quisenberry's facts and figures were one result. A series of letters to other states, asking about their land acquisition programs, was another. Garretty had been particularly insistent that Wood should try for some type of enabling legislation in the next session of the legislature. "Get a law saying the commission has the right to acquire land," he argued, "and worry about where the money will come from later."

It was good advice, Wood realized, but getting the law was more easily said than done. "Sounds great in theory," he had told Garretty, "but the legislature isn't about to pass enabling legislation if it means giving up one of its powers to the commission. But even if I knocked myself out and got a bill through, how much use would it be in practice? Everybody's in favor of saving wildlife lands; it's like apple pie, motherhood, and sunrise all together. But there ain't nobody going to want to pick up the check. Your legislation is going to be as useful as a car without gas."

For a minute longer, Avery Wood fidgeted around in front of his blackboard. He would still go for the bill, he told himself, if he could see any way of prying the legislature loose from one of its jealously held powers. But there seemed no way of doing that. Annoyed with himself for not accepting a dead end when it stared him in the face, he slouched back to his desk and forced himself to think of more immediate matters. The waterfowl season would soon be underway and he needed to

review some of the information he had collected in Mobile while
attending a meeting of the Mississippi Flyway Council, the federation
of state and federal wildlife officials that determines—not always amicably—the hunting season and bag limits for ducks migrating along the
Mississippi River watershed. Bill Holland, a Fish and Game official
from Alabama, was president that year, and he and Wood had hit it off
well together.

It was to Holland that Wood's thoughts now turned. He was remembering a conversation the two of them had one evening in Mobile,
during which Wood had mentioned his obsessive concern about preserving natural areas while there was still time. Holland had advised
him to get in touch with an organization called the Nature Conservancy, a nonprofit group that specialized in saving wild land. He had
had dealings with it himself and had gotten on well with one of its
people, a fellow named Dave Morine. Avery Wood had told him he
would think about it. However, in checking with his own staff, he had
been advised that the Conservancy, though a nonprofit organization,
charged interest on the money it used when acting for a state as a land
acquisition agent. "So what," he had growled. "Who doesn't charge
interest? Interest is what makes the world go round." Nevertheless, he
was told that the Game and Fish Commission could not deal with a
private agency on those terms. "Hell," he had snapped, "one more piece
of red tape." But he had put Holland's suggestion aside.

Now, however, it came back to him. He got up from his desk once
again and made another round of the room, ending up, as usual, in
front of the blackboard. Those numbers, representing vanished forests
and channelized streams, would only grow every time he asked Quisenberry to update them. He had no remedy of his own. Why not try this
Nature Conservancy? He had never heard of it until a couple of months
ago and for all he knew it might be some two-bit do-gooders' outfit. But
why not? There was nothing to be lost that wasn't being lost already.

CHAPTER III

The Nature Conservancy

IN A CORNER OFFICE of another building a thousand miles north-east of Jackson, Dave Morine, the Nature Conservancy's newly appointed vice-president in charge of land acquisition, was also thinking about Mississippi and the future of its natural resources. He was less restless in his meditations than Avery Wood. The office walls were of glass and he had no intention of letting the secretaries see him pacing back and forth like a bear in a cage. Besides, he had no blackboard to visit. He remained seated behind his desk, gazing at the ceiling, his manicured fingers pressed together like a steeple.

When he was a boy, Morine had been self-consciously chubby. He was very much trimmed down now but retained a square stocky build. His cheeks were round and shiny; he radiated health, cleanliness, spotless grooming—the sort of man who after hours spent in taxis, waiting rooms, and planes always looks as though he has just showered, dressed, and combed his hair minutes earlier. He was in his early thirties and the normal expression on his unlined face was one of bird-bright interest. Even when he was frustrated and tired, as now, he looked like a conscientious undergraduate studying for a difficult exam that he knows he will pass.

Morine was not at all intimidated by the responsibility of his new vice-presidential position. But he was keenly aware that the man who had previously occupied this spot—Pat Noonan, now president of the Conservancy and Morine's boss— would be a tough act to follow. During his term as chief of land acqusitions, Noonan had racked up a remarkable score, rescuing hundreds of thousands of wild acres from the threat of development, using every trick in the book to do it. Morine was determined to do as well, or better if he could. Under Noonan's direction, the Conservancy was redefining its objectives, creating new policies; and in this atmosphere of change Morine was eager to stake out some new territory for himself. Which was why he had been thinking of Mississippi, *terra incognita* as far as the Conservancy was concerned, but a potential laboratory for a concept that he and Noonan and some of the other members of the staff had begun to play with—the idea that the Conservancy should develop working partnerships with state governments as a new way of acquiring threatened natural areas.

It was Wayne Jackson who had first turned Morine's thoughts towards Mississippi. For the last six months, Jackson had been working at the Nature Conservancy, using its library to research a book he was writing. The previous week, when the two men were having lunch together, Jackson had asked Morine to look into a matter which might be of interest to the Conservancy and which was certainly of interest to him. He went on to describe his relationship with Graham Wisner and the young man's connection with the Pascagoula Swamp in southeastern Mississippi. Jackson explained that he had never seen the place himself, but he faithfully repeated Wisner's glowing description of its beauty. He also recounted as much as he knew of the Wisner family's financial interest in the Pascagoula Hardwood Company, and the plans to sell the tract.

Jackson's information was at best sketchy, and Morine had listened with growing skepticism. If young Wisner was to be believed, the officers of Pascagoula Hardwood were planning to sell the company to Masonite Corporation, one of the largest timber companies in the world, through an exchange of stock—but without first advising all their shareholders about their intentions. Jackson, relying on Wisner's information, had suggested that Pascagoula Hardwood might be a bit embarrassed if it were confronted with the impropriety of doing business in such a way. Perhaps the transaction could be stalled; and in the meantime some compensatory arrangement could be made either with

Pascagoula Hardwood or Masonite to save at least a part of the swamp from being cut-over.

Morine was pretty certain that the directors of Pascagoula Hardwood would not jeopardize the sale of their company by neglecting to notify their stockholders first. However, he agreed to look into the matter as a favor to Jackson, whom he liked and respected. A few days later he had met with one of the Masonite officials involved in the transaction and quickly learned that Wisner had indeed been mistaken. Pascagoula Hardwood had certainly notified all its shareholders, and it was not the directors' fault if the Wisner family had not advised young Graham of what was going on. More important, the sale was not pending, as Wisner had reported. It was already concluded, or would be as soon as it received the approval of the federal Securities and Exchange Commission. Since an exchange of stock was involved—Pascagoula Hardwood shareholders receiving Masonite stock in return for their own—rather than an outright purchase of the land itself, there was no way that any of the swamp could be held back as a donation to the Conservancy even if Masonite officials were interested in such an idea, which they evidently were not. Once the SEC cleared the sale, Masonite planned to pool the estimated value of the Pascagoula timber with its other assets—it had even made this provision a condition of the sale—in order to increase the value of Masonite shares on the stock exchange. Under these circumstances, company officials had not been impressed with Morine's talk of tax-deductible donations, and he had returned from the trip empty-handed.

Since he had no great expectations of success, he was surprised at the disproportionate sense of let-down he felt now that the venture had miscarried. But the reason was not hard to find. During his interview with the Masonite people he had begun to realize the scope of what was being lost. The secondhand enthusiasm of a young long-haired idealist like Wisner was one thing; hard data was something else. Morine had discovered that the Pascagoula tract was not only enormous, but that almost all of it was mature hardwood forest in a relatively undisturbed condition. Also, it was dotted by dozens of sizable lakes, and the

Pascagoula River which bisected the property was free-flowing and unpolluted. During his two years with the Conservancy, and especially while working on projects in the Southeast, Morine had learned that land like that, in that quantity, was almost impossible to find anymore.

Nor was that all of it. As soon as Wayne Jackson had begun talking about the Pascagoula, Morine, in spite of his better judgment, had begun to think of Pascagoula Hardwood or Masonite as a possible entree to Mississippi itself. If he had been lucky, if he had been able to approach Mississippi state officials with a project like the Pascagoula in his pocket, they would have had to take notice. Then maybe, just maybe, the Conservancy's new idea of working with the states could have been put to its first major test.

Nowadays, when Morine recollects his younger self in 1973—the green vice-president in the newly assigned corner office—he is assailed by a small fit of nostalgia. "We've accomplished a lot of what we only dreamed of doing then," he explains with a shrug. "Now we know what we're doing, where we're going; but there isn't the same sense of challenge. In 1973, 1974, it was the golden age for the Nature Conservancy. Everything was changing. It was a whole new ball game."

Morine is fond of hyperbole. But in this case he does not exaggerate. The early seventies were a critical period of change in the organization's history. Compared with other environmental groups like Audubon and the Sierra Club, the Nature Conservancy was almost unknown to the general public, although, as such groups go, it was a fairly venerable institution. It had evolved from the Committee for the Preservation of Natural Conditions, established in 1917 by the Ecological Society of America, its membership composed of scientists and naturalists already worried about the deterioration of the natural environment. Until after World War II, committee members got together occasionally to read highly technical papers which became more and more broadly concerned with the effects of chemical pollutants and technology on vulnerable species and ecosystems. In 1946 the committee was reconstituted as an independent organization, the Ecologists Union, which was increasingly concerned with the preservation of natural areas.

In 1951, some of the people associated with the union reorganized again, this time as the Nature Conservancy. Soon after, the group became affluent enough to purchase two small tracts in the Northeast, partly as study areas for member scientists, partly as a token expression of concern for the nation's increasing number of endangered ecosystems. This modest step had important repercussions. Before long, the Nature Conservancy discovered that it had entered the real estate business without quite meaning to. During the next two decades the organization became the recipient of hundreds of donations of land varying greatly in size and ecological value. Many were of real significance, but many others were donated, according to Morine, "by well-meaning people wanting to protect the view from their windows." The Conservancy became, in his words, "a land-grabber." Its role during most of these years was usually passive, accepting unselectively whatever came its way. Also during this period the spirit of scientific research, which had brought the organization into being in the first place, almost disappeared.

In the early seventies the Conservancy began once again to change direction. The proliferation of land parcels scattered all across the nation, rarely more than a thousand acres and frequently only one or two, was becoming a serious management problem. It was evident that a more discriminating approach to land acquisition was in order, as well as a clearer definition of what the Conservancy's purpose should be.

The search for this purpose was personified in Patrick Noonan, an energetic young man still in his twenties when he joined the Nature Conservancy in 1969. Previously he had been a land planner in Washington, D.C., first in private practice, then with the Maryland Parks and Planning Commission. He had always been interested in the subject of land use—he had a graduate degree in regional and city planning as well as one in business administration—but he found the work itself discouraging. He was "results-oriented"—a favored term of his—and soon wearied of undertaking studies and master plans that "changed every three or four years without anything ever getting done." The thought of bureaucratic red tape still makes him impatient. "Do you know," he exclaims, "that there are thousands of environmental studies just of the coastal rivers in the Northeast, and yet nearly every one of them is still polluted?"

Eventually he acquired a license in real estate brokerage. He had concluded that since land planners must deal in real estate it would be a good idea to learn what the business was all about. It was a characteristically pragmatic decision which, in his view, closed a major gap in his educational background. He remains convinced that anyone in the business of preserving wild land must have some real estate training, and he makes sure that Conservancy staff members who are involved in land acquisitions get their share of it.

Noonan, notwithstanding his practical temperament, is fond of describing his interest in the environment as emotional, not scientific. "The trout stream I fished as a boy in Maryland stopped being a trout stream almost overnight. I couldn't understand how people could let that happen. My 'conversion' was as simple as that. The outdoors and real estate were my two great interests all along, so when I read an article in the *Washington Post* about the Nature Conservancy, I was interested. Soon after that, I was hired."

Noonan started out as assistant to the director in charge of land acquisition. At that time the Conservancy headquarters was a basement office on K Street in Washington, where Noonan had to share a desk with another employee. Noonan attributes much of the organization's subsequent growth to the budgetary skills of Ed Kingman, the vice-president of finance. To Kingman also goes the credit for hiring Patrick Noonan. Within a year, Noonan had become vice-president in charge of land acquisition, the job he would presently assign to Morine. By 1973, when the then president, Ed Woodman, resigned, Noonan had made himself sufficiently important to the organization to become the first president ever chosen from the staff. At once he called upon his department heads, including several, like Morine, whom he had hired himself, to help determine the direction which the Conservancy should take in the years ahead.

"There were a hundred questions we had to settle," Noonan recalls. "We had to decide on quantifiable goals: How many natural areas could we handle? What kinds? What sort of support system did we need? How big a staff? Should we stay centralized or not?" Privately, he was convinced that most of the 12,000 nonprofit conservation organizations in the nation were lacking in specific aims, and their efforts were too often exercises in redundancy. He was determined that the Nature Conservancy would not duplicate the programs of any of the other groups. This sense of a special mission appealed to his staff, many of them refugees from the business world. Greg Low, his executive vice-president, speaks for them when he says, "It was my business school mentality, I guess, but I couldn't imagine working for an outfit that wasn't clear about its objectives. And most other environmental organizations had no planned approach."

Whether that judgment was fair or not—Low himself admits the importance of groups that are more confrontation oriented and versatile than the Conservancy—Noonan and his department heads agreed that their own approach would be as planned as possible. After fifteen months of sometimes stormy meetings, during which the staff began to think and act as a team, the makings of a five-year plan were defined (though in fact some of the policies in the plan had been taking shape while Noonan was still a vice-president). Henceforth, it was decided, the Nature Conservancy's overriding aim would be to selectively seek out and identify lands that contained exceptional biotic communities or endangered species, and then go after them. As the staff grew fond of saying, the Conservancy would be "an ecological Noah's Ark" which would preserve gene pools of flora and fauna threatened by the flood of human population and technology.

In order to pursue this more active and selective policy, the land acquisition personnel were to be trained in the intricacies of tax law, government grant programs, and the principles of buying and selling real estate. Also, the Conservancy headquarters was to be decentralized, with regional directors managing their own staffs. Even members of the Conservancy's board of directors would be expected to actively participate, using their influence to aid staff members in closing deals, as well as raising funds and setting policy.

If the Conservancy was going to initiate real estate transactions on a large scale, more capital was needed. It would be necessary to increase memberships. Furthermore, big business would have to be recruited as contributors of money as well as acreage. Acquisitions, whenever possible, were to be handed over at cost to state or federal agencies that had been unable to acquire the land themselves because of red tape or inertia. State chapters of the Conservancy would have a more active role too—they would not only identify threatened tracts, but sometimes buy and manage them themselves, borrowing the money from the national office and paying it back through their own fund-raising campaigns.

Under Noonan's leadership, and with these guidelines to follow, the Nature Conservancy has since prospered even beyond the normally optimistic expectations of its staff. Greg Low cheerfully points out that "between 1973 and 1978, just about everything has more than doubled." Memberships increased from 21,000 to 56,000. Noonan, who now tries to restrict himself to fund raising, especially corporate fund raising, has already talked more than a quarter of the largest corporations in America, the "Fortune 500," into contributing annual grants. In five years the Conservancy's working capital has grown from $6 million to $32 million. The staff has also doubled, now occupying an entire floor in a large Arlington, Virginia, office building. In particular, the number of trained scientists has grown and a new system of ecological inventory has been developed by Bob Jenkins, the vice-president in charge of science programs. There are also four regional offices with dozens of men and women in the field who act as spotters, outright purchasers, tax advisors, land stewards, or all-purpose middle men in transactions that commonly involve thousands of acres and millions of dollars. The complexity of these transactions has also increased. "We're doing deals now that we never would have dreamed of five years ago," says Low.

Although the Conservancy turns over more land than ever to state and federal agencies, the natural areas under its own supervision now exceed 600,000 acres. The only thing that has not changed is the number of deals that the staff closes each year—about two hundred, or approximately one every working day. "We could close a lot more," Low explains, "but we don't want to. It's quality, not quantity, that counts now. When I first came here, the number of acres and the market value of land we picked up was what got someone like me a promotion or a raise. Now Bob Jenkins's ecological inventory has given us a new peg to hang our hats on. Some little bog in Delaware may be more worth saving than a whole mountaintop somewhere else."

In his prescription for success, Noonan cites "focus, a plan, and teamwork," but it is the last of these that he stresses most. "Everything we have going here is a team effort," he declares. To a remarkable extent, the team is formed in Noonan's own image, a fact that most of its members would take as a compliment. They like and admire him; and the indefatigable pace he sets for them contributes to their sense of being an elite regiment in the conservation wars.

Patrick Noonan is a large man with a blazing smile, handsome in a hearty Jack Armstrong sort of way. He looks like the former athlete he is, and the raw energy he generates can become an atmosphere even in large crowded rooms. More often than not, he is on the road, with a schedule so arranged that no one trip has a single objective. It is not unusual for him to meet with the executives of four or five corporations in two states in a single day and still get home to his family by evening. The meetings are usually successful; his messianic enthusiasm for the Conservancy and its aims is highly infectious. "I was taught a person is put here to be of service to people," he says. "That's what gets me up in the morning. If I were interested in the arts or the minority issue I'd try to be of use in those fields. But my training and personal interest are in this one. Saving wild areas is tangible. I can see it; it's actually there."

However, Noonan does not let his exuberant sense of moral purpose get in the way of hardheaded negotiation. Businessmen like him be-

cause he is businesslike himself, a characteristic they do not usually
associate with environmentalists. His presentations to them are orches-
trated to appeal to their enlightened self-interest as well as their altruism.
Allusions to posterity and the common profit coexist amicably with
references to corporate profits and tax write-offs. The fact that Noonan
can combine the two activities he loves best, making deals and being
socially useful, undoubtedly accounts for much of the sense of inner
well-being he projects. "He's the most deal-oriented person I've ever
met," says Dave Morine, admiringly. "Give him a hundred dollars,
push him off a plane in the middle of the jungle, and he'll be back in
three days with a deal all sewed up and everybody smiling." Big business
tends to agree. After dealing with Noonan, one corporate executive
remarked, "The Nature Conservancy is the only [environmental] group
that follows through in a serious, business-like way."

The same combination of practicality and altruistic zeal is met in
almost all the members of the Conservancy staff. When Greg Low
claims that "guys stumble in here not knowing what they want to do,
and all of a sudden their eyes light up," it is not an idle boast. The
atmosphere in the Conservancy office is palpably invigorating. "We've
got graduates from business school, forestry school, divinity students,
even a Ph.D. in medieval literature. We're a magnet for the mutations,
the one-in-a-hundred guys who are goal-oriented but who don't want to
work for a bank or sell jello all their lives."

The professionals on the Nature Conservancy's staff have enough in
common with each other to pose for a group profile. Most are still in
their mid-thirties. They share a middle class background and were born
in the suburbs of small or medium sized towns. They come from stable,
religiously orthodox homes. Their fathers were usually self-made men,
committed to the work ethic, who often had to make financial sacrifices
to help their children through college. The children were conditioned to
help themselves. Most worked part-time during high school and college
but still found time to be Boy Scouts, class officers, school athletes, and,
invariably, good students. All of them would be making higher salaries
selling jello or working in a bank. During the troubled sixties some

taught school or joined the Peace Corps rather than go to Vietnam, but most were temperamentally conservative, repelled by the lifestyle, if not necessarily the aims, of the counterculture. Dave Morine, for example, admits matter-of-factly, "I felt some contempt for those other young people at the time. They were doing well by the system and yet biting the hand that fed them. But in retrospect, seeing what Nixon did and how Vietnam turned out, I'm glad some people had that commitment. I was brought up to respect authority. Hell, if there were only people like me in the world, we'd all be like Jeb Magruder, doing what we're told. I'm glad some people had the financial security to take the system on when it was wrong."

Nevertheless, Morine and his colleagues are unanimously agreed that as far as the Conservancy is concerned, working within the system is the only way to go. They philosophically assent to capitalism and only regret that environmentalists do not adopt its methodology more often. "The trouble with the conservation community," Morine argues, "is that there are too many people going around saying, 'I remember when—.' Hell, industry doen't give a damn about history; it continually looks ahead. So should we. I say, what's done is done." Morine is actually talking about nostalgia, not history, but his point is plain enough. Notwithstanding Noonan's vanished trout stream, or Morine's own recollections of boyhood summers on an unspoiled lake in Maine, or similar memories stored up by other staff members, the general opinion is that looking back is an exercise in futility. Morine again: "I have no patience with these guys who are always saying, 'If only we'd saved this or that twenty-five years ago.' Hell, if only I'd bought IBM stock twenty-five years ago I'd be sitting out under a tree today! What I care about is saving land right now, so kids twenty-five years from now will be saying, 'Boy, I'm glad you did that back then.'"

Even the house publication, *The Nature Conservancy News,* expresses this preoccupation—obsession, really—with the here and now. Unlike most other environmental magazines, this one contains no transcendental insights, Leopoldian meditations, laments for lost species. It presents straightforward reports of what the Conservancy is currently up to, and nothing else. This no-nonsense approach pervades all the organization's activities, and supports its view of itself as being conservation's new wave. The prevailing opinion of its professional staff, even the scientists among them, is that although the degree-carrying ecologist and the wildlife biologist are essential in providing necessary research about threatened ecosystems and species, the actual rescue of the nation's wild heritage should be left in the hands of dedicated, pragmatic people who may not know the difference between a prothonotary warbler and a canary, but who know how to make a deal.

"That's what I love about the Conservancy," says Morine, whose knowledge of natural history is no better than it should be; "it's the commitment and financial know-how that count. The biology you get by osmosis. If you give us a guy with a good biological background we have to spend two years trying to teach him the financial ramifications of a deal because the tax laws are so complex and don't really make much sense anyway. Why? Because they're invented by man and he doesn't make much sense either. Whereas if you give us a guy with a good financial background we can make him an acceptable biologist in a couple of weeks—acceptable for our purposes. The reason is that whoever made the world was a lot more logical than we are. Biological laws, unlike tax laws, make total sense." He waves his hand breezily. "You know, little fish eats big fish, big fish needs marshland to survive, that kind of thing." He chuckles, possibly wondering what his scientific colleague, Bob Jenkins, would say about his ecology-in-a-nutshell. Or perhaps it has occurred to him that little fish do not, as a rule, eat big fish.

Even before Pat Noonan moved up to the presidency of the Conservancy in 1973 and Morine took his place as director of land acquisitions, both men had begun to realize the importance of state govenment in the organization's changing conception of itself. The states were the main determinants of land use in the nation and, at least potentially, they were better able than the federal government to identify endangered flora and fauna in their own backyards. However, it was the then governor of Georgia, Jimmy Carter, who first suggested the possibilities latent in this insight. In 1972, he invited the Conservancy into his state to see what could be done about preserving some land along the Chattahoochee River. Noonan headed South, bringing Morine with him. With Carter's active participation, Noonan was able to negotiate a series of deals involving outright donation of some land on the Chattahoochee and federal matching funds to buy still more. When this trading was done, the state owned $2.3 million worth of land at an actual cost of about half that amount. Pleased by this success, Carter created a blue ribbon committee of distinguished Georgia citizens charged with the responsibility of searching out important ecological and historical sites and, with the unofficial help of the Nature Conservancy, trying to acquire them for the state. The new committee was named the Georgia Heritage Trust (with Morine suggesting the word "heritage"). Since then, the trust has added about $20 million worth of land to its holdings, for which the state paid only about $12 million. Among the tracts acquired are a coastal sea island, an intact antebellum plantation, and a forested ridge whose obscure but important claim to fame is that it supports more specimens of a rare plant called the Georgia plume *(Elliottea racemosa)* than any other spot in the world. Morine handled most of these later transactions and, in the course of the lengthy negotiations, his excitement grew. "This was the beginning of it," he explains. "Here was a state group preidentifying tracts—not just waiting for whatever came up for sale—and then telling us to go get them whether the land was on the market or not. It wasn't a very selective process, but it did involve preidentification. And for the first time a state and the Conservancy were working together, even though we had no say in the selection of lands."

Those were the official reasons for Morine's enthusiasm, but the circumstances under which the deals were sometimes conducted also added zest. "Always before we were the good guys," he explains. "Everybody was nice to us when all we were doing was accepting donations. But when we started upsetting some poorly planned, politi-

cally sensitive development schemes of some big Atlanta developers"—
he grins cheerfully—"we started getting thrown out of the office."

While Morine was busy in Georgia, Noonan went into South Carolina to engineer a transaction with the Santee Hunt Club for the
acquisition of 22,000 acres of virgin swamp and marsh on the Santee
River, a property valued in excess of $20 million. He contacted each of
the twenty stockholders in the club, most of them men of great wealth,
and arranged a donation of the tract to the Conservancy which provided the donors with a tax write-off equal to the profit they would have
received from selling the land. In a subsequent manuever, Noonan
arranged for South Carolina to use the Santee tract (to be given to the
state by the Conservancy) as its collateral in a matching funds agreement with the federal government that enabled the state to buy an
additional $4 million worth of nearby wild lands. To its delighted
astonishment, South Carolina now possessed some $24 million in
natural areas at virtually no cost to itself.

At the Nature Conservancy's suggestion, South Carolina set up its
own heritage program. This time, however, potential new areas in need
of protection would not be chosen by committee nomination, as was
the case in Georgia. Instead, a new method of ecological inventory
would be used.

In his corner of the Conservancy headquarters, Bob Jenkins, the
inventor of the new system, had been waiting for this chance.

Robert Jenkins is the resident chief scientist at the Conservancy as
well as its philosophical guru. His intimidating intelligence and specialized study tend to baffle the less scientifically oriented members of the
staff; they sometimes chafe at his emphasis on quality, not quantity, but
they are proud of him and indulge him, much as warriors in tribal
societies admire and indulge their oracles and shamans. Superficially,
Jenkins does not run true to the Conservancy type; He is not noticeably
an optimist or a wheeler-dealer; and with his bulky build and thinning
hair, his deflated cheeks covered by a bushy orange beard, he looks
older than the norm. It is even said that when he was first hired he wore
an earring in his ear. Scratch the surface, however, and he proves to be

as energetic and results-oriented as the rest. Jenkins acknowledges that the latter characteristic is not typical of the scientific temperament. Indeed, he feels that his technical concern for the methodology of ecological inventory may have made him an outcast in the academic community where the pure science of ecology is more valued than the means of applying it. "I doubt that a lot of Charles Darwin's work could be published if he were doing it today," he says sadly.

Jenkins is the creator of a system that attempts, for the first time, to objectively determine the relative ecological worth of a given wild area. His approach coincided exactly with the Conservancy's evolving decision to be more selective about the quality of the lands it was trying to preserve. Jenkins is convinced that traditional methods of determining ecological value are next to worthless. "How do you decide?" he intones rhetorically. He paces back and forth in his office with stately tread, stroking his beard. He knows the answer to his question because he invented it, but he doubts that his listener will understand. "Most wild areas are preserved by sheer happenstance. People usually begin by trying to nominate pieces of landscape that are important to them for one reason or another. Often the only criterion is beauty!" This is said with inexpressible scorn. "On that basis we should preserve all the Rocky Mountains and nothing in Kansas. When in fact, a Kansas slough adjoining a garbage dump might be more important ecologically than a scenic river in Colorado because it contains the only subspecies of some fish or water plant."

He pauses. When he contemplates the pathetic failure of previous inventories, even the most enlightened of them, we are with Lear on the stormy heath: "Almost all of them were, oh, one-man efforts," he says heavily, "labors of love, tragically underfunded, doomed to oblivion!"

Even his most devoted admirers admit that Jenkins can be a bit hard to follow at times. "Holy mackerel," Morine exclaims, "I could tell you ten stories of state people staring at him, not knowing what he was talking about. Me either. Once when he was talking to the state people in Colorado one of them actually told him to slow down. Jenkins couldn't believe it. He became so flustered he grabbed a chair for support. The chair collapsed! I'm telling you, he can be a loose cannon on a ship. But the thing about Jenkins is that he's right."

Here is Jenkins explaining the problem of determining ecological priorities: "*If*, in fact, the Nature Conservancy is interested in ecological diversity" (Jenkins is still not at all sure that some of his colleagues appreciate its importance), "then theoretically we must preserve high quality examples of the whole array of element types. This means, theoretically, that we could take all the lands in the world and sequence them—somehow—from most to least important. In order to accomplish any real preservation activity, we would then have to confine activities to, let us say, the upper 5 percent. But here's the problem. If you are an organization—as we have been—responding to opportunities as they come along, there is nothing in the system that confines those opportunities to the right part of the significance spectrum. In other words, if the opportunities are random, then 95 percent of the opportunities are not actually opportunities."

Jenkins irritably points out that although the nation has begun to be aware of the ecological diversity it is in the process of losing, there is as yet no systematic, nationwide effort to tabulate what lives or grows where, what is rare because it is localized, or what is rare because it is threatened with extinction. Bald eagles or snail darters receive attention at a moment of crisis, if at all. The federal government has still made no effort to inventory the floral and faunal elements in various ecosystems before a forest is cleared, a river polluted, or a dam built.

But even if the effort were made, how would it be undertaken? Jenkins believes that his inventory system is the answer, or at least the right approach. Briefly, he argues that ecosystems should be defined in terms of species and varieties—what he calls "element occurrences"— not in terms of natural areas. For example, instead of identifying a particular oak-hickory forest and immediately deciding that it should be preserved, one determines how many oak-hickory forests there are in a region and which are the most representative examples of the type. At the same time, data are compiled, using a computer, on various flora and fauna, particularly rare or unprotected ones, which are known or suspected to be part of an oak-hickory forest system. The result is a "search image," a hypothetical ecosystem that contains not merely an oak-hickory forest but the maximum number of "cellular elements" that are in need of protection. One then seeks out the actual geographical locality that most closely conforms to this search image, and tries to define its boundaries in terms of the habitat requirements of the endangered "cellular elements"—the flora and fauna—that are found there.

Natural areas as such, Jenkins explains, are each unique and too complex to deal with. "We have to devote our attention to things, not places. We have to take a hard-nosed statistical approach to ascertain what things are the most important part of a landscape—or rather, the search image of a landscape. Usually we decide that the most important parts are those which, taken together, viably perpetuate the greatest array of biological and ecological diversity. We've created a filtering system composed of a coarse filter of terrestrial and aquatic community types, and a fine filter composed of special species, localized and endemic as well as endangered. On the basis of this data we try to determine which part of what oak-hickory forest—or whatever—is most in need of protection. However, we might on some occasions want to protect a habitat that has only one rare or localized species on it, if it were not protected otherwise."

Jenkins's approach to ecological inventory comes complete with its own computerized system and its own methods of collecting data to feed to the computer. It also embraces the realities of political systems; and at this point Jenkins's complex, inductive mind moves in tandem with the policy that Noonan and his team of deal-makers were developing on their own, namely, that state government was the best political medium through which the Conservancy could pursue its aims. As Jenkins distinctively phrases it: "The states are small enough so that they can be encapsulated in the individual's consciousness." Besides, he adds, states are more apt than the federal government to fund inventories over a long period of time.

Now, thanks to Noonan's feats of land acquisition, a state was available to Jenkins as a laboratory. South Carolina was receptive to any suggestion the Nature Conservancy cared to make. In 1973, with the Conservancy footing much of the bill, it became the first testing ground of Jenkins's inventory system. Inevitably, there were problems. "Nobody understood what Jenkins was trying to do," Morine recalls. "Hell, after six months Jenkins announced that *he* didn't understand either. So he revamped the whole system and started over!"

Actually, Jenkins revised his methodology several times before declaring himself satisfied. But the chief obstacle to the success of the inventory had nothing to do with the system itself. Unlike Georgia, South Carolina had no single department to supervise the management of its natural resources. The South Carolina Heritage Program and the implementation of the inventory were handled by the Department of Parks, Recreation, and Tourism. However, as the Conservancy belatedly discovered, the acquisition of natural areas was chiefly controlled by the Department of Wildlife and Marine Resources, which at that time was more interested in the hunting and fishing potential of the tracts it purchased than their ecological uniqueness. As a result, there was little relation between the inventory's findings and the state's acquisition policy. "We still had a lot to learn," Morine recalls. "By the end of 1973, the inventory in South Carolina was in good shape, but the political set-up wasn't right. In Georgia we had the right kind of government support but there wasn't any inventory."

But if the heritage program was marking time in the last months of 1973, other Conservancy activities were moving ahead at an accelerating rate. Noonan had just persuaded the Union Camp Corporation to donate 50,000 acres of Virginia's Dismal Swamp to the Conservancy and he had now begun a long and complex set of negotiations that would add the state's barrier islands, one by one, to the Conservancy's Virginia Coastal Preserve, the largest and perhaps the most important refuge owned by a private conservation group. In June, 1973, Noonan became the Conservancy's president. It was an exciting time for the young staff, which was now called upon to help chart the organization's future course. The period of the organization's greatest growth was just beginning; and many of the policies described in the previous pages were still untried.

Sitting in his office on that gray November afternoon in 1973, Dave Morine was aware that as far as his new responsibilities were concerned he too was still untried. He didn't doubt his capabilities, especially now that he was beginning to have a clear idea of what "this business" was all about. He had already brought off some important deals of his own. But he wanted to test himself in some wholly new situation. He was certain that this new, half-finished concept, the heritage program, was the way to go. He believed in Jenkins's inventory system, and he certainly agreed with Noonan's frequently repeated injunction "Go with the states." The trouble was, which state?

That it would be in the South, he had no doubt. His experience in Georgia had convinced him of that. The plundered Northeast was a lost cause, at least as a model for a heritage program. And the West was half public domain already. No, the big challenge was in the New South; that was where the battle for resource allocation would be won or lost.

A few weeks earlier, Morine had written an article for the *Atlanta Constitution*. In it he had said:

During the past few years it has become obvious that a wave of unplanned development is sweeping the South. Economically this growth may prove beneficial to many native Southerners, but unless this development is controlled and directed into appropriate areas it will destroy much of the South's great natural, recreational and historical heritage. If there is anyone in the South who would like to dispute this fact, just look what has happened to the Northeast section of America . . . . Today many sections of the Northeast are environmentally dead. Every major river is polluted. The coastline is overdeveloped. The bulk of the marshland has been dredged and filled, and urban sprawl has turned most of the coastline from Boston to Washington into one big, congested, polluted megalopolis.

It is no wonder that individuals and industry in the Northeast are looking to the South for a new way of life. Unfortunately, it appears that the Northern exodus that is invading the South has learned nothing from the mess it is leaving behind and from every indication, they are determined to make the same mistakes all over again . . . . If anything, the South has already given away too much too cheaply . . . . Before it gives away anything else it should realize the value of what it has.

Rereading the piece, Morine was satisfied that it said what he believed. The question was, how much effect would it have? Not much, he decided. That was the problem with the conservation movement: being right wasn't enough. It was the degree of influence that counted. Perhaps that was why most environmental groups were always reacting to disasters instead of creating programs to prevent them. Even the Conservancy spent most of its energy snatching land out from under the developer's nose. Whatever influence conservationists had was of a kind that could only be brought to bear in a crisis situation. To Morine's way of thinking, "haphazard conservation was no better than haphazard development." But what could conservationists do? They were forever on the outside of the decision-making processes that created problems in the first place. The great trick was to find some way of being on the inside.

Morine's thoughts kept returning to the heritage program, what there was of it. If Jenkins's inventory did what it was supposed to, it would be an important step in the right direction—identifying vulnerable species before they got stomped on, instead of afterwards. And of course people like Noonan and himself had an important role, acting as ex-officio land agents for state agencies. But they were still outside the decision-making process. The more Morine thought about it, the more he became convinced that the real potential of the heritage program was in its ability to bring the Conservancy as close as it could legitimately come to initiating state policies concerning resource allocation. He wasn't sure how it could be done, but *if* it could be done it would be the first time a privately funded conservation group would be able to systematically influence policy before, instead of after, it was made.

Morine suddenly remembered the direction these thoughts were coming from—the aborted Pascagoula project . . . Mississippi. For a minute, Wayne Jackson's tip had made him hope that he had found the "new ground" he was looking for. It had been a foolish hope, he decided. Even if the Masonite people hadn't cut him off, Mississippi was not very promising as a model of the New Conservation in action. The state's Game and Fish Commission had never even bothered to respond to any of the Conservancy's earlier overtures. And there were exactly three Conservancy members in the entire state.

Morine realized guiltily that he was wasting time, a mortal sin in his book. There were a dozen other projects that needed his attention. He was about to make a phone call concerning one of them when the push key board lighted up with an incoming call. A second later his secretary was at the door. "Long distance," she announced. "A Mr. Avery Wood."

CHAPTER IV

The Heritage Program

WHEN DAVE MORINE DISEMBARKED at the Jackson airport on November 28, 1973, he was excited but also a little apprehensive. It was his first time in the state. The Mississippi of church burnings and murdered civil rights workers had been barely put to rest, and he had brought some of his preconceptions of the state along with him. When he reached the exit gate, his apprehension took palpable form. A hulking state trooper with a no-nonsense look on his face advanced on him and asked, "You Mr. Morine?" Morine fleetingly remembered the Amherst yearbook for his graduating class, which had contained a full-page photo of one of his classmates, prostrate and bleeding generously while a Mississippi state trooper loomed above him with a billy club. He clutched his attache' case tightly, gulped, and nodded. He shivered too, but that was because the suit he was wearing wasn't warm enough. He had thought he would have a respite from the northern winter, but Mississippi was gray and bitterly cold.

The trooper, it developed, was on a friendly mission. He explained that he was assigned to chauffeur Morine to the Game and Fish Commission's headquarters downtown. Morine relaxed, at least enough to notice as they drove into town that Jackson, with its new suburbs, its demolished older neighborhoods and block-long parking lots, was another Atlanta in the making. Atlanta was Morine's favorite example of what should not happen to the South.

As soon as Morine and Avery Wood met in Wood's office they exchanged a hearty handshake and a minimum amount of small talk, and began to size each other up. Both were outgoing, talkative men, but the surface resemblance ended there. Morine was the very Yankee New Englander, Wood the exuberantly friendly delta Mississippian. Morine, self-confident, usually abstentious, neat almost to the point of being prim; Wood, disheveled, impulsive, fond of cigarettes, whiskey, and late hours.

Wood, characteristically, was the first to come to a conclusion: "Soon as I laid eyes on Dave," he recalls, "I could tell that dude was Ivy League. He was articulate, astute, everything I wished I was. And on top of that I could tell he was just a beautiful guy, a prince."

Morine, also characteristically, was more cautious: "Here's this guy Avery, always moving around, very fidgety. At first I didn't know whether he was full of bull or not, whether he's in control of things. I liked him; but if I teamed up with him was I going to get myself in a jam or not? You've got to know where people are coming from before you get lined up with them in a new situation."

However, during the next several hours of nonstop talk these reservations vanished, and by the end of the day the two men were fast friends. "Avery's crazy," Morine decided, "but he's bright as hell, and I like people who are bright and want to do good things. He's not your typical state employee, or your stereotyped southerner. He doesn't get into that Civil War bull, and he doesn't make polite conversation. Right away he gets into issues. And he's got great ideas. He's a genius in his way."

As for Wood's appraisal: "I knew right away that we were going to have a little problem with Dave, because some of the people down here weren't going to care for his yankee accent, his style, you know? But by this time in the ball game I'd developed rapport with some of the legislative leaders—they'd say, 'that s.o.b. Avery may be crazy but he's no fool'—and I figured that if Morine could get their undivided attention, and I backed him up, he could sell them on whatever he wanted to do." There was no question that he had already sold Avery Wood.

Both men, aware of their temperamental differences, would later marvel at the ease with which they worked together. The friendship that evolved was always a professional rather than personal one; but since both were most wholly themselves in their professional lives it was no less deep for that. During their future partnership they would occasionally lift a glass together at a Jackson bar, and they spent countless late hours in each other's company, plotting and planning like two boys about to form a secret club. But there was never much time for personal confidences; the talk was always shop. Although they often promised each other that they would take a few days off to go fishing or duck hunting together, somehow they never got around to it.

In spite of the obvious differences in habits and temperaments, there were close parallels in the influences that had shaped the two men. Morine had grown up in Arlington, Massachusetts, a town of about 50,000 people just outside of Boston where his father worked for the State Department of Education as supervisor of vocational guidance. Even in his leisure time the senior Morine was committed to the interests of young people, proctoring their social gatherings, refereeing their games. By living frugally during the depression years, he and his wife were able to buy a home in one of Arlington's better neighborhoods, where Dave Morine and his brothers grew up, not unaware that they were "the poorest kids on the block." At the local golf course they earned spending money by caddying for their wealthier neighbors, acquiring in the process a subtle awareness that they were apart from, and more independent than, their affluent schoolmates. This independence was encouraged by their father, whom the boys revered. "He saved and scrimped so we could live in that nice neighborhood," Morine remembers, "and then he'd stay awake nights worrying how he was going to pay for it." Mr. Morine had a "depression mentality" — paying cash for everything, including the rent on a small camp in western Maine where the family spent part of each summer. The camp overlooked a mountain lake, the fishing ground not only of Morine, his father, and their few neighbors, but of a resident eagle called Old Tom by the locals. Old Tom's activities were usually an indicator of where the fish were running. In the fifties, the decline in the quality of the fishing, the increase in the number of summer homes, and the disappearance of

the eagle coincided with the awakening of Morine's ecological conscience.

Morine took his undergraduate degree at Amherst. Then, in a display
of the independent thinking his father had encouraged in him, he
decided to enroll at the University of Virginia for his MBA. "Nobody
could believe that. Nobody left New England! But I was always drawn
to the South. I don't exactly know why. The closeness to the land, the
smoother style, the images . . ." Morine waves his hand vaguely. "I
liked the country living, I guess. Many of the people at Virginia were
high-class jerks, walking around in madras shirts and tailored shorts
with a bottle of whiskey in their back pockets. But my roommate was
from South Carolina and he was great. Real down-home humor. I
became very close to him and his family. They had inherited a mannerly
lifestyle that's hard to describe." Another vague wave. "I don't know.
The southerner's real strong suit is common sense, something that's
been lost in today's world."

The more Morine speaks about the South, the more evident it
becomes that his definition of common sense has more to do with the
dictionary's "shared by all alike" than with "practical judgment." As he,
the young outsider, perceived it, the South still possessed a common,
"shared" sense of the importance of family, community, God, in the
lives of its citizens — the same institutions that Morine had been taught
to value in the vanishing New England of his boyhood. His temperamental, rather than political, conservatism attracted him to the very
region that the majority of his peers regarded as the most benighted in
the nation.

Avery Wood's parents, like Morine's, worked hard to give their
children a better life than they had had. And like Morine, Wood
considers his father the greatest formative influence in his life. The
family's rented home was on East Market Street, "the wrong end of
Greenwood," when Avery was growing up. His father was a mechanic
operating a small garage. He too was a product of the depression years,
trying to make a living when there often seemed to be more mechanics

around than cars. Sometimes Wood's mother worked behind a counter in the local department store to help her son and daughter through school. "I'd have to say my origin was humble," Wood explains, "But we weren't unhappy or anything like that." East Market Street might not have been a "good" address, but for a bright and curious boy it was an exciting place to live. Within a few blocks there was a poultry market with live geese, the railroad tracks and a hobo jungle, a couple of beer joints, boardinghouses, and, at the end of the street, the Yazoo River. There was no summer place to escape to, but there was less need of one, given the accessibility of surrounding streams and forests. Wood's father, like Morine's, found time to be mentor to his neighbor's children as well as his own. His great passion was fishing, and he often took a couple of Avery's friends with him when he and his son fished for bass or catfish in the Yazoo River. Avery's own preference was for hunting — he claims he is the best duck hunter in Mississippi — but there was time enough for both pursuits. "The important thing was being in the outdoors. It was just real relaxing, you know? My dad and me had some good times together." In order to encourage his son's enthusiasm, the senior Wood regularly did free maintenance work on a local landowner's car so that Avery could have access to the man's duck blind on a private lake.

Wood won a football scholarship to one of Mississippi's many junior colleges, and then moved on to Mississippi State. Later, he enlisted in the Navy and was sent to Officers' Training School in the Northeast. At this first exposure to the North and northerners, a less inquisitive mind might have closed up shop, but Wood found the experience exhilarating. "A lot of the guys in my company were from Harvard and Princeton and Dartmouth, real Ivy League types. I developed a real respect for them; they seemed to be one hundred years ahead of what was going on down in the country, you know?"

Most of these new companions were fairly well-read and self-asserting. The diversity of their opinions and their willingness to express them were a revelation to the small town southerner. In Greenwood there had been little intellectual outlet for Wood's boundless energy, his restless questioning, whereas here he could let himself go. These competitive young men were at ease with change; in their view "turning things around" was not only possible but an inevitable process to which one accommodated oneself as a matter of course. If Morine had discovered a shared value system at the University of Virginia, Wood was exposed, at the Naval Training School, to a greater diversity of opinion and a more activist atmosphere than he had ever encountered before.

During their first meeting, which lasted all day, Morine and Avery Wood became high on talk. Both were enthusiasts, both eager to "do something big." Wood was familiar with the rhetoric of the New South; but the rather different New South that Morine, the outsider, had in mind for Mississippi was a lot more appealing to him, not least of all because it confirmed his own views. "Mississippi's bad image has protected the state," Morine told him. "You haven't had to take the full brunt of industrial expansion — yet." True, he went on, the state had been deprived of the economic benefits of that expansion, but it had also been spared the social and environmental costs. The state still had time to chart the course that development should take — if only it would. Morine described to Wood the nation's widespread dissatisfaction with the quality of public and private life, its sense that technology had somehow gotten out of control. Government and industry were not being very responsive to this mood, he said, but it was there; even the current slowdown in the economy had not dampened it. Cities were choking with traffic, crime, and general grubbiness, and the contagion was spreading to the commuter suburbs, which in any case were neither one thing nor the other, falling between urban and rural lifestyles. No, he said, the new ideal for most Americans had more to do with the renewal of old values and the accessibility of green countrysides—the commodities Mississippi still had for sale—than with a bigger and better television set or another car in the garage. In this revision of the good life, Mississippi, always last in line, might now be first. If the state would seize the opportunity which the new age offered, it might even become the model, unlikely as that might seem, that other states would follow. It was all a matter of resource allocation, deciding where development could occur and where it could not. If Mississippi could only preserve the general quality of its environment, the quality of its way of life would preserve itself. Except that it would be better than before, because there would be more economic opportunities for its citizens, black and white. Mississippi, in short, could have the best of both worlds.

Avery Wood drank all this in like wine. It was as though thoughts that he had hardly dared to formulate were now being played back to him in the most vivid of terms. When Morine went on to explain his own tentative hopes for the Conservancy's heritage program, Wood was ready for him. "Listen," he said, "if you'll lend me your brain power, with my know-how about Mississippi and its people, we can make something happen in this damn state! We can probably do whatever we're big enough to come up with."

Morine told him about the limitations of the heritage programs in Georgia and South Carolina, as well as his ambition to see the Nature Conservancy working in close partnership with the states to secure threatened natural areas. But curiously, his thoughts were focused at the moment almost entirely in the potential of Jenkins's new system of ecological inventory, perhaps because Jenkins had recently announced that he had worked out most of the "bugs" in the methodology. Mississippi, he said, could be the first testing ground of the finished product, the first state to undertake a long-term "element specific" cataloguing of its natural resources before the full force of development hit.

Morine questioned Wood closely about the state's political and bureaucratic structure. From what Wood told him, it seemed evident that Mississippi's Bureau of Outdoor Recreation was the agency he needed to work with, not Wood's Game and Fish Commission. Mississippi BOR had the all important tie-in with federal matching funds, and the cost of the inventory would almost certainly have to come from that source. It was agreed between the two men that Wood would set up a meeting early in the new year at which Morine and his colleagues at the Conservancy could introduce the idea of the inventory to all the appropriate state agencies, but especially to the BOR.

For his part, Wood told Morine how desperately short the state was of both wildlife management lands and the money to buy them. The fact that until this moment Wood's preoccupation had been chiefly with habitat for game species, while Morine's was with the survival of entire biotic communities, troubled neither man at all. During this conversation and the hundreds that would follow, this seeming discrepancy was never discussed. The conservationist, Morine, although not an enthusiastic hunter, recognized the important role that sportsmen would inevitably play, in Mississippi and elsewhere, in the allotment of lands for wildlife. Wood, the compulsive hunter, had long since convinced himself, without remembering when or how, that a forest or a swamp was an aggregate of more than the number of deer and turkey it contained; this, even though he did not know much more about the ecology of endangered species than Morine knew about shooting game. Both men tactically understood that the same bottomland forest that harbored a trophy buck might also be home to a swallow-tailed kite. It didn't matter much if, in the effort to save such a forest, the kite rather than the buck should provide the main incentive.

Morine explained to Wood some of the techniques that the Nature Conservancy used to acquire land, the fund raising, the donations-with-built-in-tax-breaks, the matching fund deals with the federal government. Almost in passing, he echoed attorney Garretty's assertion that it was important to create a political situation, including enabling legislation if necessary, that would make the state's process of acquiring land as smooth as possible. When important tracts had been identified, Morine said, he would help "make a deal." But right now the first step was to get the inventory going.

Later, Morine would observe, "At the time I came to Mississippi, I understood the importance of the inventory part of the heritage program pretty well, but I only thought I understood the political part. I just took it for granted that the whole thing should be in the hands of

Mississippi BOR. And all the while, here's Avery, just tooling along, listening and asking questions, and he's already way ahead of me. He's already dreaming up the best possible system any state has yet devised to acquire land. He outsmarted us all."

As Morine talked, Wood's "know-how" about Mississippi had already begun to put itself to use. He realized at once that, as with South Carolina, the state had no single agency that could effectively control both the selection and acquisition of important natural areas. No doubt BOR could take care of the inventory, but there was no apparatus for handling the rest of the process. Here was Morine discussing all these ways of getting donations and matching funds, but Wood knew to his sorrow that the Game and Fish Commission was too restricted by legislative authority, red tape, and the limited political life of its director to take advantage of them. As long as that situation continued, the first step towards the rational allocation of natural resources which Morine and Wood dreamed of could never take place.

The day sped by. When Morine noticed that it was getting dark and glanced at his watch, he realized that he would almost certainly miss his flight home. Wood assured him he had nothing to worry about; he would drive him to the airport himself. Their excited conversation continued at a rate of ninety miles an hour, and Morine made his plane with two minutes to spare. When the two men parted it was with the assurance that they would soon meet again. During the days that followed, Wood communed more than ever with his blackboard, on which much of the information Morine had given him was now scribbled. "All that stuff Dave had been talking about was up there," Wood remembers, "and I'm standing there wondering how the hell I'm going to get legislation to go for it all. Morine had convinced me of what Bruce Garretty had been saying all along—that the commission didn't have enough leeway to acquire land. The legislature and the governor weren't ever going to turn loose of their authority over us, that was for sure. Then, all of a sudden, it hits me! We needed a committee, not just any old committee, but one that would give the politicians their share of the action, because without that nothing was going to happen. I would need nine members, three from the Senate, three from the House, and three that the governor got to pick. But there would be restrictions. The three from the House would have to come from the House Game and Fish Committee with the speaker of the House doing the choosing. Same thing in the Senate, with the lieutenant governor doing the picking from the Senate Game and Fish Committee, which would give them a chance to exercise some patronage, you know? And to keep the governor from vetoing the committee's proposals we'd give him the say in choosing the last three, but he'd have to choose one from each of the state's supreme court districts, which cover the northern, central, and southern parts of the state. That way, each region would get a representative. So everybody'd get a shot at appointing people to this prestigious committee, you see? As long as they had a say in its operation, they wouldn't be so likely to object to its acquiring land any way it could. And the committee would have a life of its own, independent of any agency, and outlasting political turnovers!"

Even the name that Wood chose for the new committee indicated his astute handling of down-home politics. Instead of the more exact title, the Natural Heritage Trust, which would have been Morine's choice in keeping with the programs already begun in Georgia and South Carolina, he called it the Wildlife Heritage Committee, knowing that the word "wildlife" would speak more to his fellow citizens.

"After I got it all thought out," says Wood, "I told Garretty to put the words together into a legislative bill, and that's exactly what he did. By the time Dave and the other fellows from the Conservancy came down in February, it was already in the hopper."

CHAPTER V

The Wildlife Heritage Committee

DAVE MORINE RETURNED to Jackson on February 18, 1974, this time accompanied by his boss, Pat Noonan, and two other Nature Conservancy people, John Humpke and Rick Jones. Humpke was a member of Bob Jenkins's growing scientific staff, and Jones, in keeping with the Conservancy's new policy of decentralizing its personnel, was the southeastern regional director, headquartered in Atlanta. As he had promised, Avery Wood had set up a day-long workshop attended by various state government officials who might be interested in the Conservancy's proposals, most of them from the Game and Fish Commission and the Mississippi Bureau of Outdoor Recreation. Each of the Conservancy people had a part in the presentation, a strategy that had not yet become routine: Noonan beginning with an overview of the organization's aims, Humpke describing Jenkins's system of element-specific inventory. Morine talking about land acquisition techniques, and Jones outlining the activities of the southeastern office and its potential usefulness to Mississippi. All of them chimed in to sell the idea that the state needed some means, specifically a Natural Heritage Program, to protect its most vulnerable natural areas and species. The irrepressible Avery Wood interrupted frequently with questions and comments, leaving no doubt about where he stood. But Morine and Noonan were more concerned about impressing the Mississippi BOR people than Wood and his Game and Fish Commission staff since it was the former agency that could put Jenkins's inventory to the test. At this time, the U.S. Department of Interior was requiring Mississippi and other states to come up with a Statewide Comprehensive Outdoor Recreation Plan (SCORP) in order to justify the infusion of federal dollars for recreation, and it was Morine's intention to have the state's BOR include the cost of the inventory in its plan. "You've got to remember that we were selling this ecological inventory idea and the whole concept of heritage programs out of the back of a truck," he explains. "There is no program at the federal level that recognizes and funds the protection of important natural areas on that basis."

From an environmentalist's point of view, determining which ecosystems and which species of flora and fauna are most threatened by development, and then protecting them before that development can occur, seems so resoundingly logical that it comes as a surprise to learn that when the Nature Conservancy conducted this Mississippi workshop in 1974, the concept had never been entertained in the United States at any governmental level, except in the experimental Conservancy programs set up in Georgia and South Carolina during the previous year. (At this writing, there is still no federal commitment to such an approach in spite of the conflicts that have arisen between the provisions of the Endangered Species Act and the proponents of federally funded projects.) Even at this meeting in Jackson, the scope of what the Nature Conservancy was proposing was missed by some of those present, partly because it was so encompassing in its simplicity, but more, perhaps, because the Conservancy speakers stressed the specifics of the program, particularly the methodology of the inventory system, which was the part of the heritage concept that Dave Morine was most intent on selling.

Throughout the session, Morine kept his eye on Rae Sanders, the head of the Mississippi BOR liasion office and the chief architect of the state's SCORP proposal. It would be Sanders who decided whether the inventory went into the plan or not. He was a quiet, blandly well-mannered man, considerably older than the four brisk northerners who, at Wood's invitation, were so free with advice. During much of the meeting he had to absent himself to take care of other matters, but even when he was on hand he left much of the questioning to his alert assistant, Cy Vance. He himself wore the attentive but reserved look that one meets in bank officials when asking for a loan. He had a high forehead with thinning hair, and a long, bejowled face that seemed melancholy even when he smiled. The blue eyes peering through horn-rimmed glasses were hard to read. When he nodded occasionally, Morine couldn't tell whether he was agreeing with a point or merely being courteously attentive. Morine, who took some pride in his ability to "size up" the people he dealt with, was baffled by this quiet, inscrutable man, and fretted about the impression that he and his colleagues were making.

At the end of the long meeting, when other Conservancy officials headed home, Morine stayed on. He and Avery Wood had a trip to Laurel scheduled for the following day. That evening the two men resumed the marathon discussion they had begun at their previous meeting. Morine, still woundup after the day's presentation, did most of the talking. Again he reviewed the successes and failures of the heritage programs in Georgia and South Carolina for Wood's benefit, and in doing so, ended by understanding their significance better himself. There were three elements that were essential, he declared, if such a program were to succeed in Mississippi: The implementation of the inventory system; the establishment of a sympathetic political set-up for land acquisition; and an important land acquisition project that would give the Conservancy credibility in the state. Morine, uncertain of Sanders' reaction, had to content himself that the workshop was at least a step towards the first objective. As for the second, although Wood briefly mentioned his current efforts to get a bill creating a Wildlife Heritage Committee through the legislature, Morine was scarcely listening. His thoughts were already leaping ahead to the third goal, the all-important project. He had never let go of the thought of the Pascagoula tract, of what it might do for the Natural Heritage Program and the Nature Conservancy's reputation if he could win some part of it for the state. Though not much given to intuition, he had a hunch that he and that impressive wilderness were not done with each other yet. He was determined to try for it one more time. As he told Avery Wood, a project he must have, and the Pascagoula was the only one in the state that he knew anything about.

Early the next morning the two men were aboard a small state plane, enroute to Laurel where both the Pascagoula Hardwood Company and the southeastern division of Masonite Corporation had their offices. With them was Bill Quisenberry, whom Wood had chosen as his aide in his dealings with the Conservancy. Quisenberry's face paled when he learned that they would travel by plane; he had a phobia about flying. Nevertheless, he obeyed Wood's summons, and spent the mercifully short trip throwing up into one or another of the bags that, prudent as always, he had brought along for that purpose. From time to time, Wood and Morine offered him well-meant raillery and useless advice, but for the most part they were too excited to empathize with their miserable fellow passenger. Morine was enchanted with the beauty of Mississippi from the air. Compared to most other states in the East, it was an unfolding map of verdant green, especially in this southeastern quarter. Great swatches of pine forest extended to the horizon, their faintly undulant surfaces traveled by small herds of cloud shadow. Sometimes when the plane passed above a creek or stream, light reflected not only from the waterway itself but from an undersurface of water among the trees.

Wood was delighted with Morine's delight, but he conscientiously pointed out the new roads and the development that followed them, the large lakes which were in fact man-made reservoirs drowning thousands of acres of bottomlands, and especially the immense, straight-edged swaths of forestland, trimmed as by a pair of shears, which were actually even-growth pine plantations in which very little could thrive except the pines themselves. Even so, Morine's enthusiasm was not to be dampened. "It's still a beautiful state, Avery," he exclaimed above the roar of the engine and the sound of Quisenberry being sick. "It would be a crime if you make the same mistakes we did!"

At Laurel, a state trooper was waiting to drive them to the Masonite plant, said to be the largest plant under one roof in the world. Certainly it was the most enormous lumber operation Morine had ever seen, columns of smoke belching into the sky, vast shadowy spaces echoing with the shriek of machines cutting wood, the sickly sweet scent of pulp in the air—all of it reminding the visitor that southern hills and swamps, not western mountains, supply the nation with most of its timber products.

Mickey De Grummond, Masonite's regional vice-president, met the three would-be deal-makers in the small outbuilding that housed his office. They had scarcely gotten past the introductions, however, when Robert Hynson, the dapper, gray-haired president of Pascagoula Hardwood, happened to drop by and was invited by De Grummond to join the discussion. The news they had to offer their three visitors was crushingly disappointing. Although no reference was made to the final ruling of the Securities and Exchange Commission, De Grummond gave them to understand that the sale had been completed and the Pascagoula Swamp was now the property of Masonite. Morine wondered in that case why Hynson was there at all, but this was hardly the time to ask prying questions. Instead he asked De Grummond to consider any one of several ways in which at least part of the tract could be protected—outright purchase, a donation with accompanying tax write-offs, a combination of both, or at the very least some sort of leasing arrangement with the state. De Grummond assured him that none of these suggestions was feasible.

As a consolation prize of sorts, he suggested to Morine that he might want to look at several thousand acres of river swamp that the company owned over on the other side of the state, in the Pearl River Basin. Since the land hadn't much economic value, perhaps something could be worked out there, a lease arrangement if nothing else. But as soon as Morine showed some interest in the suggestion, De Grummond seemed to repent of having made it. He abruptly switched the subject to a small Masonite tract just south of Jackson, where, he said, the Game and Fish Commission might contract for an annual lease. Morine tried unsuccessfully to turn the conversation back to the Pearl River. He was still talking when he and his friends found themselves out on the street.

For Dave Morine, the return flight to Jackson was a stark contrast to the outward bound journey just two hours earlier. "We're screwed," he muttered gloomily to Wood as the plane took off. "They've given us the runaround."

The quixotic Wood was less easily discouraged, partly because the interview had confirmed his opinion of Morine. Later he would say, "Here was Dave, real nice and polite, asking De Grummond for thousands of acres of land, exploring the tax shelters and all that, bold as you please, and there's De Grummond, not believing what he's hearing, obviously thinking this guy must be nuts. A guy with a Boston accent coming all the way down here to try to pull a stunt like that! It boggled my mind, I can tell you. Right then, I made up my mind that if Dave had that much nerve, he'd do to ride the river with."

As for Quisenberry, having lost his breakfast on the way out, he had nothing else to lose, but he still felt terribly queasy. As far as he could see, his never very robust stomach had been martyred for nothing.

During the months following this expedition, Morine and Wood pursued their separate ways. Morine gave his attention to Rae Sanders and the Mississippi Bureau of Outdoor Recreation. Not long after he returned from Laurel, he wrote Sanders that "Mississippi should develop a Heritage Program that will identify, acquire, and provide a management plan for the significant recreational, natural, and historical areas within the state. The problem with creating such a program is that there is no one department within the state that is concerned with all these resources. As a result, there are at the present time many independent and fragmented programs going on . . . . It is quite obvious that the logical group to coordinate all the independent governmental agencies and private groups, if any, is the BOR Liaison Office."

Even as Morine was composing this memorandum on March 11, 1974, Governor Waller was signing SB 1857 which created the Wildlife Heritage Committee. The bill was authored by Senators Donald Strider of Charleston and Sam Wright of Clinton. Both men were key figures in the successful passage of the bill and each would later be appointed to the Committee. Morine knew of the bill's passage, but because of his inexperience with the state's political process he still did not understand its significance. He continued to regard the BOR Liaison Office as the only agency that dealt regularly with the other state natural resource departments, and the only one that could fund a heritage program. Best of all, Rae Sanders had come down on Morine's side.

After the Conservancy workshop, Sanders did not keep Morine in suspense for very long. Cautious by temperament, he had nevertheless recognized at once that the proposed inventory system could be one of the most useful methods of managing natural resources ever devised. Sanders, unlike Wood, was no gifted amateur in public office. Governor Waller had appointed him to his present position, but Sanders had had long years of previous experience in the bureaucratic labyrinths of state government and had developed a feel for what could and could not be done. The inventory, he was pretty certain, belonged in the former category. To an unusual degree, he had managed to escape the bureaucratic blight that afflicts so many agency chiefs—the compulsion to protect and expand their own bailiwicks even at the expense of the real function they are supposed to fulfill. Although he was unlike Avery Wood in almost every other way, Rae Sanders shared with him a determination to do his job well. He had already been the chief architect in designing a bill to rehabilitate and maintain Mississippi's badly neglected state park system and had helped persuade the legislature to turn loose an unprecendented $20 million for the project. That bill, as Sanders would later point out, had an influence that reached beyond its immediate intent. It was the first major appropriations bill of its kind in Mississippi's history; and although it did not involve the purchase of additional lands for the park system, it had the effect of preparing Mississippians psychologically for the more radical appropriations scheme in which Wood and Morine would soon be deeply involved.

Sanders and Morine worked together to get the state's ecological inventory underway, following the new "element specific" principles that the Conservancy's Bob Jenkins had developed. During the next year Sanders would risk his own credibility by backing the process, including its expensive computer components, with substantial sums of BOR money. Although Jenkins had announced that he had finally eliminated most of the "bugs" in his cataloguing system, no one else could be sure of that. It would be up to Mississippi, and Sanders, to prove that it would work.

Eventually Bob Jenkins and Sanders would deal directly with each other in implementing the inventory (BOR would contract with the Nature Conservancy to undertake its initial phase). During the early stages of the program, however, Morine acted as go-between. Meanwhile, Avery Wood was recommending candidates to Governor Waller for the three positions on the new Wildlife Heritage Committee that were within Waller's purview. Wood and Quisenberry were also busy designing rules and procedures for the committee, and establishing criteria for acquiring land. During that March and April, Morine was in contact with Wood whenever he visited Mississippi, but he was still too absorbed with BOR and the inventory to pay much attention to what his friend was up to. "That wildman Avery was ahead of all of us," he would admit later. "He'd been tooling along, getting all the information he could out of me—just sitting there, wheels spinning, smoke coming out of his ears, listening to all the techniques the Conservancy had used—and now, while I'd thrown all our chips in with BOR, he had incorporated all the stuff he'd learned into his Wildlife Heritage Bill. It's a work of genius; it created the most comprehensive and independent government land acquisition agency in America today. It gives the Wildlife Heritage Committee the right to buy or sell land, accept donations, raise money—anything it has to do to acquire land. And Avery's doing this on his own, you understand. He made it politically viable by devising the way the committee is selected. And even though I didn't understand what he was up to because I didn't understand political realities in Mississippi, it coincided with what I was trying to do."

Important as it was, the creation of the new committee was not Wood's only coup during the spring of 1974. As matters stood, the Wildlife Heritage Committee had very little in the way of operating expenses, and Wood now cast about for a way to solve that problem.

He soon realized that the only available source was the frozen funds from his own Game and Fish Commission. Each fiscal year, the commission was required to begin with a zero balance and then generate its own operating income from the sale of licenses, fines, and other revenues. Because of the month-to-month uncertainty about what that income would be, the commission was compelled to maintain a surplus whenever it could. As a result, the end of each fiscal year found the agency with some funds left over. This money was then frozen in a special account; that is, it could not be used by the commission except for a specific purpose approved by legislative act.

Ever since he had become director of the commission, Wood had chafed at the necessity of going before the legislature every time he had need of this money, which had been generated, after all, by the commission itself. Now it occurred to him that the Wildlife Heritage Committee not only could use these funds, but could supply him with the means of getting at them. He approached Charles Deaton, acting chairman of the House Appropriations Committee and chairman of the House Game and Fish Committee. Both men were natives of Greenwood and had known each other all their lives. Like Wood, Deaton was in his early forties, but he had already become one of the most influential men in the Mississippi House of Representatives. He was also a strong supporter of environmental legislation. He had been indispensible to Rae Sanders in getting the $20 million allocation for the rehabilitation of state parks, and more recently he had guided Wood's Wildlife Heritage Committee bill through the House.

It would be uncomfortable to ask a man who had just helped him to help him out again, but Wood decided that if Morine could be "as brazen as a Times Square hooker," so could he. He asked Deaton to sponsor a bill that would transfer the frozen funds to the Heritage Committee where they would be used as the committee saw fit. Deaton lifted his salt and pepper eyebrows. He started to point out that the legislature had done Avery Wood enough of a favor for one session and that in any case it would be in no mood to surrender any more of its authority, least of all where money was involved. But Wood argued that the House and Senate between them had six out of the nine members on the committee. Since that was the case, wouldn't the legislature still have control of the money and what was done with it? Deaton grinned; Wood's argument was hard to refute, especially since Deaton had arranged to be appointed to the committee himself. After giving the proposal some thought he told Wood he would go along with him. Not long after, the necessary bill was passed.

"Lo and behold," crows Wood, remembering, "in a few months we not only had enabling legislation to acquire land but a $700,000 kitty. And when you figure that the money was matchable three-to-one with the feds' Pittman-Robinson funds, we were good up to $3 million, which was beyond my wildest dreams. Damn, I felt good about that!"

It was fortunate for Avery Wood that he could feel good about something. During the same months when his public life was proving so exhilarating and challenging, his private life was coming apart. His wife, whom he had first met while she was still a student at Ole Miss, was now an alcoholic, and it was necessary for her to be hospitalized for considerable periods of time. The responsibility for their two children, a nine-year-old boy and a five-year-old girl, was wholly Wood's. In spite of his delight in his work and his devotion to his son and daughter, there were often painful conflicts between family responsibilities and professional ones. Governor Waller, one of the few people in Jackson who knew of the problem in the Wood household, was supportive; and Wood's old Greenville friend Bill Barrett and his wife, as well as one of his cousins, became at times surrogate parents for the two children. But it was a strained and often unhappy period. Although Morine and Wood didn't talk much about personal matters, this domestic problem was sometimes self-evident. "Avery was forever calling home to see about baby-sitters, or to tell the maid something, or to see that his boy got to a football game. When he could make it, he'd hurry home to fix the kids' dinner himself. You could tell this thing ripped him up pretty bad, but he never let it get in the way of his work. The commission, the Heritage Committee—they were the most important things in his life. I think maybe they were what kept him going."

The first meeting of the Wildlife Heritage Committee, in the spring of 1974, had been concerned with organizational matters. The second, on July 10, 1974, was the first one that Morine was able to attend. By this time he was beginning to appreciate the committee's potential importance. As yet, he had no official status in the state but he had become a familiar face in the governmental circles in which Wood and Rae Sanders moved. With their sponsorship, the Nature Conservancy's real but unauthorized voice in the state's environmental concerns was beginning to be taken for granted. Morine had made himself liked. He was intelligent and earnest without being too self-asserting; he had an engaging smile and knew when to laugh at other people's jokes. Even his Boston accent and Ivy League manners did not present the problem Wood had feared they might. He was so obviously a Yankee, yet one who did not look down on Mississippi and its citizens, that his very Yankeeness became a point in his favor. When he arrived at the meeting some of the committee members greeted him more as an ex-officio member than as a guest.

Morine is still apt to describe his impression of the assembled group in the gee-whiz terms of his New England boyhood: "I was just a visitor so I sat against the wall, not at the table. When I looked around I saw all those big cigars, the ducktails, knit leisure suits and white shoes, and I thought, holy mackerel, what have I gotten myself into! I'd never seen so many impressive Faulkner types in one room before. I was wondering what a New Englander like me was doing in a crowd like this."

The "crowd" might have been impressive, but the setting was not. This was the conference room of the Game and Fish Commission on the third floor of the Robert E. Lee Building. Two former hotel rooms had been joined into a single long narrow chamber, the original bathrooms still intact. A threadbare rug covered the floor, and the mismatched chairs around the conference table looked as though they had been picked up at a Goodwill sale. The room faced the façade of Jackson Central High School, with a view of the room in which the school band regularly practiced. On this occasion and many others, committee members found themselves competing with Sousa when they tried to speak.

Avery Wood sat at the head of the table, with Bill Quisenberry at the other end taking the minutes. Next to Wood was his ally in the House, Representative Charles Deaton, smoking, as usual, a large Belvedere Dutch Master. He was handsome enough to be a matinee idol, tall, with a commanding presence and deep voice, keen blue eyes, and prematurely graying hair neatly waved and curling at the neck into a modest ducktail. Even his political opponents conceded that he was an expert politician, and many of his admirers felt that he came as close as Mississippi legislators could get to statesmanship. More than once during the next two years, the fortunes of the Wildlife Heritage Committee would depend on his decisions.

Beside him was Senator Ray Montgomery, crippled, in a wheel chair, also smoking a cigar. He was heavyset, wore horn-rimmed glasses, and was famous for getting anywhere he wished to go in spite of his disability. For a Mississippi senator, he was not at all flamboyant. He spoke rarely, and when he did, in a soft voice. He would almost never miss a committee meeting, and Wood particularly liked him because conviction, rather than expediency, usually governed the way he voted.

The second of the senators, seated across the table, was "Son" Rhodes, an outgoing, back-slapping man with a voice which, unlike Montgomery's, could be heard a long way off. He was short, bald and along with his colleagues, brandished a big cigar. By all accounts he enjoyed being a senator immensely and knew how to play politics. His home was Vancleave, on the edge of the Pascagoula Swamp. In much of the committee's work he did not participate very actively; Wood, although he liked him, worried sometimes about his reputation as a politician. As it turned out, Wood's fears were unfounded. In at least one of the crises that lay ahead for the committee, Son Rhodes's help would prove invaluable.

Next to Montgomery sat Don Strider, Wood's most influential

supporter in the Mississippi Senate. In Dave Morine's opinion, he was the archetypal southern politician, rather floridly dressed, with a thick Delta accent, long, reddish hair combed back behind his ears, and an impish smile. He chewed his cigars without ever lighting them. In terms of political power, he was, in the Senate, the committee's counterpart to Representative Deaton in the House. On more than one occasion, Avery Wood would count on him to sponsor important legislation.

The other two politicians at the meeting were Representatives "Farmer" Jim Neal and Tommy Gollott. When not being a politician, Neal was the most popular disc jockey in Jackson. He had a morning show, and it was said that people in the area did not get up until he told them to. Surprisingly, however, his personality in the committee room did not match up with the stereotype of either his political or radio roles. He was thin, almost gaunt, and rather shy in manner—perhaps the most unobtrusive man in the room. If he had any competition in that last respect, it came from Tommy Gollott, another thin, quiet man in a room filled with extroverts. Gollott represented the Biloxi area and had a moving business on the Gulf. Along with Deaton and Representative Lynn Havens of Gulfport, Gollott would later author HB 914 authorizing $15 million for the purchase of the Pascagoula tract.

The remaining three men on the committee were Governor Waller's appointees, Bill Allen, John Vaught, and Bruce Brady.

Allen had been elected the committee's chairman for the first year. As the owner of the largest Mack truck distributorship in the world, he was by far the wealthiest man in the room. Allen was well-groomed in a dapper, Johnny Carson sort of way, wearing a very large, crescent-shaped diamond ring and an agreeable smile that made him look younger, and less shrewd, than he actually was. He could be amiable and considerate—Avery Wood was grateful for the moral support he gave him during this period of marital stress—but it was generally agreed that he was not a man to cross. He was also Governor Waller's best friend. Waller trusted Allen and listened to his advice; on that count alone he was one of the most influential of the committee's members.

Easily the most famous person sitting at the table was John Vaught, the most successful coach in Ole Miss's football history. Though in his sixties, he kept himself tanned and trim. Morine was impressed by the fact that he was much more soft-spoken than he had expected the coach of one of the toughest teams in the Southeastern Conference to be. In Mississippi he was considered "a living legend," "a way of life," and he was always surrounded by admirers. Even high-ranking politicians were apt to sidle up to him, asking how the team was doing, or whether he could possibly find an extra ticket or two for some visiting cousins.

Of all the members of the committee, Bruce Brady was perhaps the most intellectual and the most informed about ecological and environmental subjects. His family was impeccably "Old Southern" and his father was a well-known author and judge. Brady himself had studied law, but was by preference the southeastern editor of *Outdoor Life*. He was one of the few people on the committee who dressed conservatively; he wore a large moustache, eyeglasses, and had the look of a scholar. Wood had particularly asked the governor for this appointment. Although Brady spoke rarely during committee sessions, he was listened to when he did. He was an "idea man," and he had access, through *Outdoor Life*, to a great deal of research information which the committee would put to good use.

To a considerable degree, the Wildlife Heritage Committee's make-up would change with time. But during the months that lay ahead, these were the men who had to make the sometimes difficult decisions that would set its permanent course, and, in the process, create one of the most innovative conservation programs in the nation.

From Morine's point of view, the July meeting of the comittee began well enough. Wood discussed the sums of money that had been transferred from the Game and Fish Commission's frozen funds to the Wildlife Heritage Committee's account. Then Morine was invited to speak of the possible uses to which they could be put. Morine enthusiastically described the importance of preserving the state's most unique and vulnerable natural areas as well as some of the means of achieving that end. This was the first time that any of the voting committee members had heard the Nature Conservancy's views on ecological "gene pools" and selective land acquisition, and they listened with careful interest. When he was finished, Morine congratulated himself that the message had come across.

But the next item on the agenda, introduced by Senator Strider, was something called Grassy Lake. Even now, Morine pronounces the name in the same tone that a union official might use for right-to-work.

Grassy Lake was located in Tallahatchie County, Senator Strider's home territory. In its day the lake had been famous for its fishing, but in recent years it had deteriorated due to agricultural pollution and aquatic growth. Some of Strider's constituents wished to see its productivity restored, and Strider felt obliged to do his best for them. As chairman of the Senate Game and Fish Committee he had earlier tried to convince the Game and Fish Commission to reclaim the lake, but Wood had pled an insufficiency of funds for the project. However, now that the Heritage Committee had been created—with a lot of help from Strider—for the express purpose of acquiring lands, the senator was ready to try again. His constituents were convinced the lake could be a recreational showplace and they were pressing him hard to rehabilitate it. This meeting was as good a time as any to bring the subject up. The committee had some money, after all, and this seemed a good way to spend it. So Strider explained the proposed project to his fellow members and recommended it for study.

Morine sitting in the background and obliged to keep his mouth shut, realized to his dismay that the committee was listening to Senator Strider just as attentively—and sympathetically—as they had listened to him. It wasn't that Strider was behaving irresponsibly; by traditional standards, Grassy Lake was an acceptable project. But Morine had gone too fast for his audience; he had supposed that when he talked about the importance of natural areas and ecological diversity, everyone had been with him. It was a shock to discover that his understanding of those terms and the committee's were so unlike. As far as he was concerned, "Senator Strider's proposal meant stepping back to square one, a return to conservation's Dark Ages. We'd just created a space-ship and instead of heading for the moon, these guys wanted to go to the corner drugstore. It was selection by random nomination all over again, and with political expediency the decisive factor. In short, it was exactly the sort of approach to land acquisition that the Nature Conservancy had been trying to outgrow." Glumly, Morine wondered if Avery Wood's new committee was going to amount to anything after all.

The committee agreed to study the Grassy Lake proposal, and soon after, the meeting adjourned. As soon as Morine had Wood to himself, he bewailed the turn that the meeting had taken. Wood heard him out but refused to share his agitation. He told his friend that he was expecting too much too soon, that they would all have to learn as they went along. In the meantime, Morine should leave it to him to keep Strider's proposal at arm's length. He even confided his suspicion that Strider himself, though bound to support the project, would not be broken-hearted if it came to nothing.

During the months that followed, the members of the committee would indeed learn as they went along. But it was also true that the Grassy Lake project—"that crummy little pond" as Morine called it—did not go away. As Wood predicted, nothing ever came of it, but it continued to appear on the agenda of committee meetings, sharing equal billing with issues that Morine considered infinitely more important, reminding him always of the direction in which the heritage program must not be allowed to go.

During his conversation with Wood, Morine lamented, "If only I had a real project to give them, then they would see the difference." Four days later, when Morine was back in his Arlington office, he received a call from Graham Wisner. It was the first time that the two men had been in direct contact with each other. Jubilantly, Wisner told him that the Pascagoula Hardwood Company had just advised its shareholders that the Securities and Exchange Commission had refused to approve some provisions for the exchange of stock between the company and Masonite. The Pascagoula sale had fallen through.

CHAPTER VI

"Like A Pure Young Woman"

ON THE EVENING of August 26, 1974, Graham Wisner and Dave Morine shared a taxi from the Robert E. Lee Building to the Jackson Airport. Morine was silent, thinking over his own part in the day's events. He looked uncharacteristically shaken and subdued. For awhile Graham Wisner watched him from the corner of his eye, grinning wickedly. Then he said, "Tell it to me again, Dave. I want to hear how Mississippi is like a pure young woman." When Morine answered him with a drop-dead look, he broke into a repertoire of chortles and giggles that went on for the rest of the drive. Morine cursed silently, but he admitted to himself that there was justice in Wisner's gloating.

The two men had met for the first time the previous evening at the Washington airport. Events had moved quickly since Wood and Morine had learned that the Pascagoula sale to Masonite had been called off. Morine had phoned Wood, saying, "Let's shoot the moon on this, Avery." Wood hardly needed encouraging. He had at once set up a general meeting to sell the Pascagoula Swamp project to Mississippi's officialdom. Wildlife Heritage Committee members, Game and Fish officials, and representatives of other important state agencies were invited. Governor Waller said he would be there. It occurred to Morine that it might be a good idea to ask Graham Wisner to attend the meeting. It would be helpful to have one of the owners on hand to sing the praises of the swamp and urge the state to come rescue it. He called Wisner, and the young man said he would be glad to cooperate.

When they met for the first time at National Airport, however,

Morine began to have second thoughts. Although Graham had made the rare concession of dressing-up for the occasion, he managed to look as far-out as ever. "When I saw him, I nearly dropped," Morine recalls. "Here was this guy in an ultra-mod continental suit, double-breasted jacket with high shoulders, bell bottom trousers. And long hair! I wanted a clean-cut all-American kid who would talk about hunting and fishing, and I get the personification of the liberal Eastern Establishment, bleeding heart causes written all over him. Jeez! I just knew he'd blow us out of the water."

The sizing-up worked both ways. Graham could spot a "square" as quickly as Morine could spot a well-tailored hippie. Furthermore, he was pleasantly aware that under the circumstances he had the whip hand. On the plane, the two men had seats in first class because those were the only tickets Morine had been able to get at short notice. The liquor was free, and Morine imbibed more than he usually did. "The more I drank, the more nervous I became. I realized Graham was too smart for me to control. He had my number better than I had his, and he played up every stereotype I'd ever had of Mississippi. He took a fiendish delight in telling me what he was going to do. I spent the entire flight hearing about all the injustice Mississippi had heaped on its people, and how Graham was going to use the meeting to tell the governor what he was doing wrong. By the time we got off the plane I could hardly walk."

Morine assumed that Wisner, at least, was enjoying himself. In fact, the young man's raillery was a form of bravado, meant to conceal worries of his own. He wasn't concerned about what the Mississippi officials might think of him, but he dreaded the reaction of his relatives if they got wind of his expedition. He would make no false claims when he gave his talk, but he knew that all those politicians and bureaucrats would assume he was representing his family's views. It was uncomfortable to think of what Bob Hynson, the Chisholms, even his own brothers, would say to that.

The next morning, the two men went to the state capitol where a number of important state officials were already gathered. As soon as

Governor Waller entered, Avery Wood introduced Morine, describing him in extravagantly glowing terms. Morine stood up. He had a speech prepared for the occasion, as well as maps and charts. By this time he felt that he had developed an ear for the southern taste in rhetoric and he was eager to try it out. "Mississippi is unique among the eastern states," he began, "because she still has a chance to determine her own destiny. She is still rich in natural and human resources which Industry from more exploited parts of the country is only beginning to discover. Mississippi is like a pure young woman with her whole life still ahead of her. Her virtue must be protected. She should be looking for a lasting relationship with Industry, one in which she will remain an equal partner by preserving her dowry of natural resources, rather than allowing Industry to squander it." Here Morine paused for effect. Then: "If Mississippi allows herself to be raped by Northern Industry, as the Northeast has been, she has no one to blame but herself."

The silence following this sentence was broken by the scraping sound of a chair being pulled back. The governor was getting to his feet. Without a word, he left the room.

Avery Wood puffed furiously on his cigarette while staring at the lighting fixtures overhead. Quisenberry's normally pale face became pasty white. Various department heads, not knowing what else to do, cleared their throats and coughed. Wisner, from the far end of the conference table, gave Morine a smile which explicitly said, "You dummy, you." Morine himself stood there for some time, feeling, as he would later explain, like a man who has been knocked unconscious and didn't know it yet.

Governor Waller, it must be remembered, was a staunch advocate of industrial expansion. He was currently using every means at his disposal, including generous tax breaks, to lure northern industry into the state. He was also a strongly opinionated, forceful man who did not like to be contradicted. "I figured Waller took my speech as a slam against himself," Morine recalls. "His *modus operandi* was to tell industry to come and get it; and I'm saying, 'Don't give it away.' When he left the room I was aghast. I stumbled around for a few minutes, burping and

farting, trying to get through my speech while everybody looked embarrassed."

He was still trying when the door opened and Waller reappeared and
took his seat again. The governor looked around, surprised at the
sudden silence. "Sorry," he said. "There was an important call I had to
make. You all can begin now." He had been so preoccupied with his call
that he had not heard a word Morine had said. Morine, voice shaking,
started over, this time deleting all references to Mississippi's chastity.

In contrast, Graham Wisner's performance went smoothly. He
stressed the beauty of the Pascagoula, and his strong personal hope that
the state would acquire it and preserve it as it was. He was soft-spoken
and respectful; and later, when he was asked questions, Morine was
surprised at the number of "yessirs" and "nosirs" that accompanied his
replies.

When Morine and Wisner had made their presentation, the governor, who was listening closely now, asked, "All right, what do you want
us to do?"

Morine, his composure regained, suggested that a resolution be
drafted instructing the Game and Fish Commission and the Wildlife
Heritage Committee to explore the possibility of acquiring the 42,000-
acre tract for the state. Waller agreed and the resolution was quickly
passed. Morine was delighted. Although the Nature Conservancy had
as yet no official status in Mississippi, he knew that his credit was still
good with the Heritage Committee and the Game and Fish Commission. With Avery Wood backing him, he would have a free hand to take
on the project, which was as challenging as any he could have wished
for.

Before leaving for the airport, Wisner and Morine spent several
hours with Wood and Quisenberry, planning their next moves. Wood
was beaming. "It's like fate or something was bringing it all together,"
he said. "First Graham and his idea about saving the swamp, then the
Masonite deal falling through, then me dreaming up the Heritage
Committee, and now you, Dave, with your financial know-how. We
can't lose." Even the cautious Quisenberry shared in the general eupho-

ria. And until he and Wisner headed for the airport, Morine was able to forget his exercise in southern eloquence.

During the next months, events moved quickly. Avery Wood asked for, and got, endorsements for the project from every state agency that was concerned with natural resources. He sent Quisenberry and the commission's public relations man, Melvin Tingle, into the Pascagoula Swamp to make a film. He discussed with Representative Charles Deaton how best to get a legislative appropriation for the purchase of the swamp, a subject somewhat complicated by the fact that the value of the tract was not yet determined. By October, when the Heritage Committee met again, a roughly edited twenty-minute version of the Pascagoula film was ready and was shown for the first time. Committee members were enthusiastic and gave their official approval of what was now the Pascagoula Project; every effort would be made to acquire the property, even if no one was quite sure yet how it would be done. Morine was at this meeting, but all that he remembered of it later was that Grassy Lake shared the agenda with the Pascagoula. Senator Strider, who had been as enthusiastic about the latter project as everyone else, now pressed again for the reclamation of his local lake. "Avery managed to sidetrack it," Morine growls, "but nobody stood up and said, 'Look, we don't have time for this.' Just mentioning those two projects in the same breath was sacrilegious to me. It was ironic that for the next two years, of all the projects in America, the one I liked most and the one I liked least were always on the same agenda."

However, by this time, Morine and Wood had more pressing matters than Grassy Lake to worry about. While Quisenberry and Tingle were in the Pascagoula making their film, they had noticed teams of professional timber cruisers working the swamp, taking estimates of its standing timber. A little investigating determined that the men were working for International Paper Company, and that a sale might soon be pending between that company and Pascagoula Hardwood. This was a crushing discovery to Quisenberry. The swamp's beauty had impressed him deeply. Carried away by Wood's and Morine's enthusiasm, he had allowed himself, against his better judgment, to believe it might be saved. Now he swung to an opposite extreme, assuring Wood that all was lost. "IP is the biggest timber company in the world," he groaned. "Pascagoula Hardwood will never be able to refuse. In another year the whole tract will be clear-cut."

Avery Wood told Quisenberry to go back to work and leave the worrying to him. Then he phoned Morine, who flew to Jackson at once. The two of them quickly enlisted the aid of Bill Allen, the chairman of the Heritage Committee and, more important, Governor Waller's closest friend. Allen, though an affable man in his more relaxed moments, possessed a powerful ego and a determination to have his own way. Wood admired him and was grateful for his support both professionally and in the matter of his disintegrating marriage, but he often said of him, "Bill's a great friend to have, but I'd rather cross Carlos Marcello than cross him." Now when Allen heard of the problem posed by IP, he frowned. He had committed himself to the rescue of the Pascagoula and it annoyed him to see that commitment threatened. "We'll go to the governor," he said, reaching for his phone.

A little while later, Morine and Wood trooped after him to Waller's office. Allen did most of the talking: International Paper was planning to buy the swamp. The swamp was Mississippi's first-last great chance to protect its natural heritage. Would the governor ring up Sanford J. Smith, the chairman and chief executive officer of IP, and ask him to postpone any potential deal with Pascagoula Hardwood for awhile, long enough for the state to make an offer? Waller hesitated, then agreed, though not without first fixing Morine and Wood with a look that suggested they had better deliver the goods. He picked up his gilded phone, with "The Governor" inscribed on the receiver, and told his secretary to put through the call.

Soon after this, IP withdrew from negotiations with Pascagoula Hardwood. However, Morine didn't wait for the outcome. Next day, October 16, he headed south to Laurel, in a Game and Fish Commission car driven by Bill Quisenberry, to meet with the officers of Pascagoula Hardwood. Except for the brief encounter with Bob Hynson at Masonite a few months earlier, this would be his first contact with the company and its directors. It would certainly not be his last. During the next two years he would get to know the road between Jackson and Laurel so well that he would recognize every house and barn and Baptist church along the way.

This time it was all new. It was a fine autumn day. Morine, still not altogether free of his Yankee preconceptions about Mississippi, enjoyed the idea of seeing it from the "safety" of an official car. He didn't even mind Quisenberry's "old lady" driving. The usually reticent Quisenberry opened up to his questions and told him as much as he knew of local points of interest: the little town of Raleigh, which each year hosted a contest to determine the tobacco spitting champion of the world; the "Free State of Jones" (Jones County), which was supposed to have declared itself an independent country during the Civil War because it had as little liking for the Confederacy as the Union. According to Quisenberry, it was still the home of "some of the most independent cussed people in the world."

A visiting architect had once described Laurel as a place that "out-New-Englanded New England." But by 1974 it could have served more appropriately, in Morine's view, as a model of what lack of planning, and the wrong kind of planning, could do to a once pretty and dignified southern town. Its original business district, characterized by painted brick storefronts, high curbs, and sidewalks shaded by overhanging canopies, had been wholly altered. Acres of parking lots surrounded isolated clumps of service stations, fast food outlets, and shopping centers indistinguishable from those in the suburbs of Los Angeles, Chicago, or New York. A modern skeletal arcade disfigured what was left of the downtown streets. Morine reflected that the bulldozed town was the urban equivalent of what would happen to the Pascagoula Swamp if modern planners and modern technology had their way.

The Eastman-Gardiner Building posed a striking contrast to everything around it. In front of its high iron fence, the street was suddenly plunged into the shade of overhanging oaks. The building itself was Italianate, with three tall archways in the brick façade and enormous doors so heavy that when the lightly built Quisenberry first tried to pull one open he was almost jerked off his feet. Inside, the enormous marble waiting room, with its high counter like a bank's and its ornate wooden benches, was empty. This was Wednesday afternoon, when traditional southern businesses shut down for a midweek break. Morine had persuaded Mr. Hynson to make an exception of himself and Quisenberry when he phoned for an appointment, but the secretaries and clerks had not been kept overtime on that account.

While waiting for someone to appear, Morine reviewed the more factual information that Graham Wisner had supplied about his Laurel kindred. His great-grandfather, Silas Gardiner, accompanied by his younger brother, George, had settled in Laurel in 1891. They had been in the sawmill business in Iowa, but when the great midwestern forests were played out they headed South, as did most knowledgeable lumber men of the time. In Laurel they bought a small mill, several thousand acres of land, and soon began to prosper (so much so that in 1912 the surviving brother, George, could order the construction of the stately building in which Morine and Quisenberry now cooled their heels). In the sand hills of eastern Mississippi, newcomers did not have to compete with the descendants of planter blue-bloods for social distinction; the families which the brothers founded soon became, and remain, as close as Laurel comes to a resident aristocracy. Besides their timber interests, the Gardiners and their offspring acquired interests in banking, real estate development, and, in the 1940s, oil. Compared with these other business interests, the Pascagoula Hardwood Company had never been a major operation. Indeed, it was not founded as a family business in the first place. In 1926, when the South was already experiencing the depression that would soon overtake the rest of the nation, George Green (George Gardiner's son-in-law) and other public-spirited members of the family bought the Pascagoula tract as a civic-minded enterprise. They sold shares in the new company to many Laurel residents and set up a mill in the town to stimulate its economy and provide employment. However, the venture was not successful. Timber from the swamp had to be shipped north to Laurel by rail, when in fact the only economically feasible approach was to float it south on the Pascagoula River. In the early thirties, the company went broke. In 1935 it sold perpetual cutting rights to Mengel Corporation at depression prices, hoping to get enough of a return to pay land taxes and thereby hold the company and the tract together. But during World War II, when lumber was at a premium, the contract was the cause of understandable bitterness on the part of Pascagoula Hardwood shareholders: Mengel was cutting out timber at one-sixth its real value. In the late 1940s, the contract was finally broken and Pascagoula Hardwood again resumed control of the swamp forest, some of it still in virgin stands because of its relative inaccessibility.

During much of the fifties and sixties, Pascagoula Hardwood annually extracted several million board feet of lumber from the property, but this was not enough, apparently, to provide significant dividends to shareholders. Also during this period, several descendants of the Gardiner brothers or members of their families—chiefly the Hynsons and the Gardiner Greens—consolidated their interests in the company by buying out other shareholders who had large blocks of stock. By the late sixties, when other lumber companies began to express interest in buying the tract, the extended family controlled about 70 percent of Pascagoula Hardwood's assets. During the next few years, while the board of directors tried to decide whether to sell or not to sell, all timber cutting ceased. It was during this peaceful interlude that Graham Wisner had begun his weekend visits to the swamp.

Morine's ruminations were interrupted by Bob Hynson, the president of Pascagoula Hardwood, who emerged from a side door looking as trim and fit in his small gray moustache and tailored suit as Morine remembered him from their brief meeting at Masonite the previous spring. Hynson ushered them into the company's conference room which, like the building itself, was meant to impress visitors with its conservative elegance. The original furnishings were still in place: walnut and cane chairs surrounding a circular table, a marble fireplace and two rolltop desks, a brass spittoon, a Vernay chandelier overhead and, on the marble floor, a large bright rug woven in Puerto Rico especially for this space.

"Stem" of Upper Rines Lake, one of some fifty oxbow lakes in the Pascagoula project area. These lakes are what remain of the old Pascagoula River channel. New lakes will be formed in the centuries ahead as the river continues to change course.

Area managers Thomas H. Kirkwood (left) and Herman W. Murrah stand beside one of the large cypress trees that are scattered over the Pascagoula tract. This specimen is twenty-eight feet in circumference and estimated to be approximately one thousand years old.

Canoeist enjoying an outing on Black Creek. Approximately thirty-five miles of frontage on both sides of the creek were acquired. The creek, one of the most beautiful natural streams remaining in Mississippi, affords excellent fishing, boating, camping and bird watching.

March 11, 1974, marked a milestone in the history of conservation in Mississippi, when Governor William L. Waller signed Senate Bill 1857 creating the Wildlife Heritage Committee. Charter members of the committee were: (seated) Senator Ray H. Montgomery; standing left to right: Commissioner Bruce H. Brady; William Y. Quisenberry, III, director of the Wildlife Heritage Program; Avery Wood, Jr., director of Conservation; Representative James H. Neal; Representative Charles M. Deaton; Commissioner William H. Allen; Representative Tommy A. Gollott; Senator William C. Rhodes. Committee members not shown: Senator Donald B. Strider and Commissioner John H. Vaught.

Governor Waller announced the Mississippi Heritage Program in August 1974. Left to right: David E. Morine, vice-president and director of Land Acquisition for the Nature Conservancy; Patrick F. Noonan, president of the Nature Conservancy; Dr. Skip Lazell, Mississippi representative of the Nature Conservancy; and Avery Wood, Jr.

On April 3, 1975, Governor Waller signed House Bill 914 authorizing the issuance of $15 million in General Obligation Bonds to purchase the Pascagoula Hardwood Company lands. The Bill was authored by: (left to right) Representative Lynn Havens, Charles M. Deaton and Tommy A. Gollott.

Others present when House Bill 914 was signed were: (seated) Ray H. Montgomery; (standing left to right): Senator Corbet Lee Partridge, Charles M. Deaton, Tommy A. Gollott, James H. Neal, Lynn Havens, Senator Ellis B. Bodron, Representative Robert G. Huggins, William C. Rhodes, Senator Fred M. Rogers and Senator Thomas W. Hickman, Jr.

Transfer of the deed to the Pascagoula Hardwood Company tract from the Nature Conservancy to the Mississippi Wildlife Heritage Committee on September 22, 1976. Seated left to right: Bruce Garretty, Mississippi Special Assistant Attorney General; Dick Trauwig, legal council for the Nature Conservancy; David E. Morine; and Commissioner Donald W. Cumbest. Standing left to right: William C. Rhodes, Avery Wood, Jr., William Y. Quisenberry, III and Senator Sam W. Wright.

Graham Wisner (left) and David Morine discuss the Pascagoula project at the national headquarters of The Nature Conservancy in Arlington, Virginia. Mr. Wisner, a stockholder in the Pascagoula Hardwood Company, was the first person to approach the Nature Conservancy about seeking a way to preserve the company lands.

Robert C. Hynson (left), former president of Pascagoula Hardwood Company, and Gardiner Green, Sr., whose family controlled 25 percent of the stock in the company. They are sitting in the conference room of the company headquarters in Laurel, Mississippi.

Anglers enjoying bream and bass fishing on Lower Rines Lake. Some fifty oxbow lakes comprise approximately two thousand acres of the Pascagoula tract.

Around the table were seated six people: Gardiner Green, the company's vice-president; his son, Bill; Hynson's son, Bobby; the elder Green's sister, Anne Reeder; his cousin-in-law, Mary Cox, and Denton Gibbs, a director and the company's local counsel. Morine, accustomed by now to the committee meetings in Jackson where politicians and other self-made men predominated, was struck by the different ambiance of this gathering, which tended to reiterate the cool reserve of the setting. No cigars were brandished here, the men's shirts were button-down, the women's clothes expensive and in fashion. A round of formal introductions was made, heads nodded slightly, faint smiles appeared and then disappeared on noncommittal faces.

It was obvious at once that none of these people knew anything about the Nature Conservancy. After Morine had described the organization, its aims, and its interest in the Pascagoula, there were a few polite questions, but the listening air seemed to say, "Very well, but what has this to do with us?" Morine was beginning to wonder about that himself. Like all shrewd traders he could quickly sense the degree of interest he was generating. Here there was none at all. These people, he realized, were a buyer's nightmare: sellers who really did not much care whether they sold or not.

He plunged on, talking fast but ingratiatingly. It was not the Conservancy, he explained, but the state of Mississippi that wished to acquire the Pascagoula tract, which it would preserve for the benefit of generations to come; and so forth. He then introduced Quisenberry, as the state's representative, who confirmed the state's interest, and described the Wildlife Heritage Committee's plans to ask the legislature to provide the purchase price. At this several eyebrows around the table were raised, and Gardiner Green asked how the legislature could be expected to provide the purchase money when no one, including the officers of Pascagoula Hardwood, knew what the value of the property was. Quisenberry was a little shaken by this remark, but asserted that since Masonite had considered $15 million a fair price, the state was thinking in terms of a similar amount. "But Masonite was offering an exchange of shares," said Green. "Any outright purchase, if we were to consider it at all, would have to take into account the federal taxes on capital gains."

"Mr. Green," Morine interjected, "it would be premature for us to discuss money just now, though we hope your company will soon arrive at an asking price. For the moment, we would merely like to ask the company to give the state a year's option to buy."

There was a small silence, soon broken by Hynson. "Mr. Morine," he said amiably, "Mr. Green's point is that the company is not likely to find a cash transaction attractive, certainly not at a price that the state would be willing to pay." Neither he nor anyone else present made any reference to International Paper's interest in the company, which Governor Waller was in the process of discouraging.

During the remainder of the meeting, the display of courteous interest was maintained, but it was clear to Morine that he wasn't getting anywhere. His original perception had been correct: these people were not really sure whether they wanted to sell to anyone, and even if they did they clearly felt that the state couldn't meet their price. "What they were politely telling us," Morine remarked later to the crestfallen Quisenberry, "was to buzz off."

While goodbyes were being said, and Quisenberry was already heading for the door, Morine noticed Gardiner Green watching him through his steel-rimmed glasses. Green's skin was soft and papery, and gathered in finely wrinkled folds around his eyes, concealing their expression. As Morine remembers it, Green unexpectedly drew him to the side of the room where a large aerial map of the Pascagoula tract was displayed. Different sections were in different colors, denoting those areas of the property that were in hardwoods and those in pine. "Now, Mr. Morine," he said, "you should know that I, for one, am not interested in selling either to the Nature Conservancy or the state for cash, and I and my family own quite a bit of the stock, 24 percent to be exact. But I am interested in retaining the pine woods"—here he pointed to several colored patches along the edges of the tract—"and you, I take it, are interested in the swamp. What you must do, if you're really serious, is approach those who want to sell separately, and work out some sort of arrangement from there. That would be the way I would think of doing it."

Morine thanked Green for the advice, but by his demeanor he made it clear that he was not going to follow it. It was important that these people realize that he was as determined—and stubborn—as they; when he talked about an option to buy the tract, he meant all of it. He was not going to have his great project nibbled down to an assortment of odd-sized parcels. Receiving this message, Green gave him a dry smile and left him with the elder Hynson who showed him to the door.

Two weeks later, on the first of November, 1974, Morine mailed a formal proposal from the Nature Conservancy to Hynson, asking for an option to buy 100 percent of the Pascagoula Hardwood Company's stock for $15 million. On November 30 he met with Hynson and Green again, but both of these men, who between them represented more than 40 percent of the company's stock, seemed less receptive to the thought of selling, if possible, than they had been at the first meeting. Perhaps they had already heard of the governor's intervention with International Paper. At any rate, a week and a half later, on December 12, Hynson wrote Morine a letter saying no to everything he had proposed.

CHAPTER VII

In The Swamp

THE PASCAGOULA SWAMP, the prize for which Morine, Wood, and Quisenberry were about to experience two years of dyspepsia, insomnia, and the sometimes exhilarating, sometimes frightening sense of living beyond their selfless means, continued with its own agenda of growth and decay, registering time in terms of seasons and the rise and fall of river water. Like all southern swamps, the character of this one was—is— profoundly withdrawn; it does not invite the public gaze. A person can stare up at a mountain or down from it, look across a plain or a desert, peer into a canyon or out of a valley; the Pascagoula offers no large views of any sort, unless one happens on the occasional open lake or sunlit bog; and even there, there is the powerful sense that what one cannot see is even more interesting than what one can. As in some run-down mansion created for the purpose of Gothic fiction, there are corridors with sudden turns, rooms with shutters drawn, closed doors, secret passages, holes in the roof, and the drip of leaky drains. (Descriptions become Gothic too—murky imitations of Edgar Allen Poe. It is not surprising that no important poem concerns a swamp.)

In spite of its otherness, there is nothing to be afraid of in the Pascagoula unless one insists on getting lost or stepping on a cottonmouth. Nevertheless, the density of living forms and their inclination to infiltrate each other's positions can be a cause of wonder and uncertainty. Land there is not always solid land, water is not always altogether water. The owl perched in that tree is in fact a tangle of spanish moss. That gray drowned root is a snake. Even the most serious of the swamp's admirers admit that, while it is a wonderful place to visit, they wouldn't want to live there. With one notable exception: Herman Murrah, who would not wish to live anywhere else.

Having spent all his life in the Pascagoula, Murrah is immune to any sense of its mystery. Even its beauty is too everyday to be much noticed. It is simply a part of his life. "I love this swamp," he says. "I just enjoy getting out in the afternoon and visitin' an old lake where it's peaceful and you can't hear trucks and things. I call it a swamp, but of course it's not a swamp to the point where you can't get out and walk around in it sometimes. We gather mayhaws and muscadines and blackberries— last spring we made enough jelly to do the whole family through the winter."

In 1974 Murrah was a state game warden for the whole county, but much of his patrolling was in the deepest recesses of the swamp. He liked his work, though he cheerfully complained that "they don't pay me near what I'm worth." He was proud of being on familiar terms with the Pascagoula tract and liked to show it off. But on the morning of August 7, 1974, when Murrah was summoned to nearby Lucedale to meet two important visitors and give them a tour of the swamp, he was somewhat mystified. One of the pair was Bill Quisenberry, a Game and Fish official whom he had never met; the other was his acquaintance of four years earlier, Graham Wisner, whom he had never expected to see again. Since Murrah knew nothing of the effort to save the swamp, he wondered what these two could have in common.

By the time Quisenberry and Wisner arrived in Lucedale, they were wondering the same thing. Their meeting had been arranged by Avery Wood when Wisner, delighted by the news of Masonite's withdrawal from the sale of Pascagoula Hardwood, had volunteered to introduce state Game and Fish officials to the swamp. Wood explained that he himself would be too busy to go along, but he would send Quisenberry as his representative to meet Wisner at the Jackson airport and accompany him on the tour. Wood had a somewhat inflated idea of Wisner's importance as a shareholder in Pascagoula Hardwood, and he was more interested in keeping the young man happy than in Quisenberry seeing the swamp. When Quisenberry asked how he would recognize the man he was to meet, Wood told him, "You'll spot him right away. He'll look like a rich hippie." And, he added, "Be nice to him, for God's sake. Even if he comes off the plane buck naked, remember, he's on our side."

Graham Wisner was fully dressed, in a fashion reminiscent of Che Guevera. As Wood had promised, Quisenberry quickly spotted his lanky figure among the businessmen and homeward bound vacationers filing down the ramp. Wisner was not quite so quick to recognize Quisenberry. He had expected a middle-aged, official-looking personage. Whereas, although Quisenberry was actually Wisner's senior by a few years, he could be mistaken at first glance for a teenager. He was slight of build, and his small, sharp features were set in a lineless face. The expression in his eyes was one of cosmic rue, but even this made him seem young in a war-orphan sort of way. Wisner was a little annoyed. "Here I was offering to show the swamp to these state people," he explains, "and all they send me is a kid."

The drive down to Lucedale did nothing to improve on this first impression. When conversation came around to social issues, the two men quickly discovered they were on opposite sides. Quisenberry deplored racial injustice in Mississippi but politely blamed the northern liberal establishment—which Graham Wisner almost flagrantly epitomized—for much of the recent turmoil in the state. Wisner, as inevitably, advocated socialist solutions to current problems, all the while wishing his companion would drive a little faster.

Herman Murrah was waiting for them at the appointed place, a cafe on Lucedale's main street. After Quisenberry had been introduced and Murrah and Wisner had brought each other up to date over a cup of coffee, they climbed into Murrah's jeep—Quisenberry in the back, which had no padded seat—and began their tour. They crossed the Pascagoula River west of Lucedale and headed south for several miles along the ridge that edged the swamp. Unexpectedly, Murrah pulled over to the side of the road, unlocked an inconspicuous gate, and drove through. Beyond, the descending lane led first through pine lands, then a hardwood forest. The air was gray, heavy with pending rain. On either side, the wall of trees occasionally opened on a view of small ponds where wood ducks paddled among the table-sized stumps of cypress trees.

Quisenberry questioned Murrah about the area's wildlife. Alligators were present, he was told, but just barely. Murrah admitted that in earlier decades he and his father were among those responsible for nearly exterminating the species, sometimes killing dozens in a single night. As for black bears, a few might still survive on the tract, though he hadn't seen one himself for many years. Panthers were supposed to be extinct, but Murrah was convinced they still held out in the area, having heard their unearthly cries during some of his nocturnal patrols. Quisenberry expressed skepticism about that. There was no authenticated evidence that the animal survived anywhere in the state; on the other hand, he knew that woodsmen clung wishfully to a belief in the panther's continuing presence, confirming it every time they heard the yowl of a love-sick bobcat.

The prospect was more cheerful for the area's deer herd. Murrah recalled that when he was a boy deer were so scarce "that if you found a track you'd bring the whole family to look at it." But in the Pascagoula, as elsewhere in the South, the animals had been restocked and were now thriving in spite of heavy hunting, legal and otherwise. As though to submit itself in evidence, a doe materialized on the road ahead of them for an instant, then gathered itself for a leap and as suddenly disappeared.

Presently the river came into view; Murrah pointed out a small island that for several hundred yards seemed to divide its course. "Just a few years ago," he explained, "that land wasn't an island at all. It used to be part of the opposite bank. The whole river came around this big loop in front of us. But all the time the current is lookin' for an easier way. It's always changin'. It keeps cuttin' corners, takin' short cuts. Now this loop is just backwater; the current is all on the other side of the island. What you got here is an oxbow lake in the makin'. Before long it'll be cut off from the river except in high water. I tell you, this river is changin' all the time."

Beyond this overview, the road returned to the forest and led to another gate which Murrah unlocked. On the other side the woods were darker, the trees taller and of greater girth. The track was barely visible; during the subsequent journey, it would sometimes vanish altogether at a fallen tree or a seemingly impenetrable thicket, only to reappear again a little further on. Murrah knew where it was, however, even when it didn't know itself. He drove the jeep forward with a manic verve, taking it over smaller logs and around bigger ones, in and out between the trees, through flailing underbrush, and up and down the banks of muddy sloughs, offering a running commentary on the passing scene which Wisner and Quisenberry, shielding their faces against the lash of branches and the certainty of being overturned at any moment, barely had a chance to see. By the time they came to a halt at a steep gully that had suddenly opened in front of them, Quisenberry's official consciousness was aghast that a state vehicle, not to mention official visitors, should be submitted to this kind of abuse. Besides, his posterior was sore from the cushionless ride. However, Graham Wisner seemed to be enjoying himself, and since his own instructions were to humor him, he held his peace—except to remark that if a man didn't have hemorrhoids at the beginning of such a ride, he would surely have them at the end of it.

After the roar of the jeep's overworked engine, the silence that now descended was all the more impressive. Even the papery rattle of the geological survey map that Quisenberry unfolded seemed excessively loud. Murrah pointed out their present position and indicated the route they would follow. The boundaries of the 42,000-acre tract were only approximately sketched in, but it was apparent that the general outline of the property extended north and south in a relatively narrow band, about twenty-five miles long and four miles wide, on either side of the Pascagoula River, which coiled back and forth upon itself through the center of the map, sometimes heading back north in its more extravagant turns. The bottomland forest, indicated by large splashes of green, was dotted by dozens of oxbow lakes with names like Hog Pond, Bilbo Dead River, and Wells Lake, as well as innumerable streams and creeks, some of the latter without any names at all. According to Murrah, the stream bed in front of them was Smith's Cutoff, which showed on the map as a barely visible line heading jaggedly for the river.

It was decided that they would explore on foot for a while. Wisner, eager to recapture the experience of his earlier days in the swamp, went barefoot. Murrah eyed him with tolerant amusement; Quisenberry, unaccustomed to the consciousness-raising rites of the hippie world, was faintly shocked but again said nothing.

For some distance they followed the twisting course of Smith's Cutoff through what appeared to be an untouched wilderness. Now, at midsummer, the stream was at its lowest stage, in places barely visible under piled-up jams of trees which its high water current had undermined. "You wouldn't believe it now," said Murrah, "but in winter the flood comes right up to the top of this gully"—they were ten or twelve feet above the stream's bed—"and some winters it spills over. Everywhere we're walkin' is covered with water, sometimes deep enough so as you can come in amongst the trees in a johnboat." Wisner and Quisenberry looked around them, trying to imagine these woods filling up with water as a northern forest might fill up with snow.

At intervals, the cutoff broadened out, sometimes into a shallow slough inhabited by impressive stands of cypress, sometimes into boggy pastures of summer grass stippled with sunflowers, pitcher plants, and the brilliant red of leopard lilies. Beyond the ravine, the bottomland woods—water oak, cherrybark oak, hickory, sweet gum, red maple, wild pecan—extended into a dim green and blue haze. Quisenberry was impressed. He had visited enough of the state's wild areas to realize how singularly unspoiled this wilderness was by comparison. If it was not virgin forest, it was close enough. The girth of many of the trees was enormous, the roots a mossy tangle supporting beds of ferns, oyster mushrooms, and catbriar vines as thick as his wrist. The canopy overhead had to be at least one hundred feet above them.

The wildlife was discreet but not invisible. In particular, squirrels were everywhere, more than Quisenberry had ever seen outside a city park. At one point a barred owl, at another, a red-tailed hawk, flew heavily away among the trees. There were glimpses of two or three more deer, their white tails bobbing distantly. From overhead came the hysterical cries of pileated woodpeckers, which Murrah called Indian hens. Along the bank of the cutoff, prothonotary and myrtle warblers, yellow-billed cuckoos, and tohees were abundant.

At several places, the three men paused to examine shallow beaver ponds. In building these impoundments, the beavers had sensibly avoided the cutoff itself, where their dams would have been swept aside by winter floods. Instead, they preferred low depressions in the adjacent woods in which rainwater could accumulate. Murrah remarked that although most of the swamp's beaver population seemed content with dens in the banks of their ponds, some built lodges along the edges of the larger streams and the Pascagoula itself. However, since these structures were left high and dry in summer by the retreating water, he guessed that they were only occupied during the winter months when the annual flood swirled up around them. Quisenberry was particularly interested in a series of large shallow pits gouged in the edge of one of the ponds, the wallowing place of razorbacked hogs. Murrah remarked that the animals were still fairly common in the swamp, though much less so than in earlier days when there were no fence laws and the beasts could win new recruits from free-ranging herds of domestic swine.

The walk continued for more than an hour. If Wisner's feet hurt him during that time, he was careful not to complain. At times there was the patter of intermittent rain adding to the humid atmosphere, but only a few drops penetrated the dense roof of leaves above them. Eventually, the forest ahead opened out, and below lay the scimitar curve of an oxbow lake. "Goff Dead River" said Murrah. "Good fishin' but not too many people get in to it. In high water you can boat in from the river, but in summer you got to walk in if you come at all."

Out on the still surface a small black spot that might have been the head of an otter or a mink suddenly disappeared. Overhead, several e-grets and a great blue heron flew by. The curving shore was neatly edged by a narrow phalanx of tall cypress, three or four trees deep. Beyond, the bank rose sharply to a height comparable to the ledge on which they stood, nearly twenty feet above the lake. Atop the bluff the bottomland forest stood as a dense wall, as it did behind them. Again Murrah reminded them that in six months time the overflow of the Pascagoula River would enlarge and deepen the lake, climbing the steep clay banks, sometimes spilling into the forest that now was high and dry. Quisenberry was particularly interested by this hydrological feature. He knew that most of the large swamp-bottomland ecosystems that survived in the South did not possess this strikingly distinct interface between "dry" forest and wet swamp. In most of them, especially this close to the coast, the line where land left off and water began was indistinct, a matter of inches of elevation, at most a foot or two. Whereas here, although the true swamp with its standing water and cypress and tupelo trees wound its way into every corner of the Pascagoula's immense hardwood forests, the latter, at least in those places where the changing river had thrown up imposing bluffs, held itself aloof. Except during the wettest seasons, it could hardly be called "bottomland" at all.

After a few minutes' rest, the men moved on. Murrah had led them away from Smith's Cutoff before they reached Goff Dead River, and now Wisner and Quisenberry no longer had any idea where in the great forest they were. "I hope you know, Herman," Quisenberry muttered, getting a cheerful laugh for an answer. A short while later they found themselves on the banks of the Pascagoula River. Even in summer, and in spite of its short length, it was a strong-looking river, the gray wide current moving between the eroded banks at a noticeably swift speed. Directly at their feet a small creek fed into it, trickling past a pile-up of broken tree limbs. Various of these had become resting places for a half dozen turtles, a large water snake, and a small cottonmouth, none of them aware of the spectators peering at them from above. Quisenberry eyed the assemblage with more than routine interest. Before leaving on this expedition, he had been briefed by one of the naturalists in Rae Sanders's BOR liaison office, and especially admonished to be on the lookout for a species of turtle, the yellow-blotched sawback, which, although rather common in this river basin, was to be found nowhere else. Quisenberry did his best to spot the tell-tale "blotches," but the turtles were a little too distant and their shells too caked with mud to make identification possible.

In time, when Sanders's ecological inventory had gotten underway with an assist from the Nature Conservancy, Quisenberry would learn that the swamp contained a host of other threatened, rare, and endangered flora and fauna—from obsure shrubs and plants like the golden canna, the odorless wax myrtle, and the green fly orchid, to the rainbow snake, the Atlantic sturgeon, and the yellow bat. (As well as the southern panther, if a single, respectably documented sighting counted as evidence enough.)

Apart from the panther, Quisenberry might not have been able to identify any of these marvels even if he had walked right past it. However, at that moment a rarity did present itself which he recognized at once. Sailing into view against blue-black clouds was a swallow-tailed kite, one of the South's most beautiful and threatened birds. Even among that most handsome and imposing of avian families, the raptors, none is more elegantly shaped or strikingly marked than the swallow-tail. Seen from below, it appears as a wintery X against the sky. No contrast could be more extreme than that between its white head and breast and black dipped wings and long forked black tail. Unless, perhaps, it was the contrast between the bird and its surroundings. In the lush untidiness of its swamp habitat the kite's stark, geometric beauty seemed almost willfully bizarre, as though it were defying all one's expectations—and Darwin's rules—about what a bird in such a setting should look like.

While the three men watched, the kite remained poised for a moment above and in front of them, so close that they could see its head turning this way and that as it searched for a small frog or snake. For a moment it seemed to be watching the watersnake and the cottonmouth, but then, perhaps because it saw the men as well, it made the slightest gesture with its wings, glided forward, and disappeared.

Wisner exclaimed that he had never seen such a bird during his earlier visits to the swamp, and Quisenberry emphasized how rare they were. But Murrah assured them that in the Pascagoula, at least, they were frequently seen soaring above the river, sometimes eight or ten together.

At that moment it began to rain in earnest. For a while on the walk back, the forest canopy offered some protection but by the time they reached the jeep they were drenched to the skin. Murrah asked if they should head back to Lucedale. The question was addressed to Quisenberry, who said no. Wisner, tempted by the thought of a dry set of clothes, was not greatly surprised by this answer. During the morning's hike he had been reluctantly impressed by Quisenberry's dogged, serious interest in everything Murrah showed them, and had concluded that the fellow was not such a kid after all.

On the trip back to the highway, Murrah had no choice but to drive carefully. The lane was becoming a muddy trap in which again and again they were on the verge of being mired. They finally made it to the blacktop, but the relief that Quisenberry and Wisner felt did not last long. As soon as they recrossed the bridge over the Pascagoula, Murrah eased the skidding jeep down another track as perilous looking as the one they had just escaped. At that point even Quisenberry may have wondered if he had not been too stubborn about wanting to go on.

The rain, at least, was reduced to a thin drizzle, and the track, once it entered the woods, held to fairly firm ground. Murrah explained that he was taking them to Hudson Lake, another oxbow, located only a couple of miles from the highway and bridge. Presently its iron surface, reflecting the gray sky, became visible through the trees. Murrah said that only a few days earlier he had received a tip that some fishermen had caught an alligator in a gill net on this lake. When he investigated, there were no people around but he had found a dead four-foot alligator, and for good measure, a dead beaver too. At this recollection, his good-natured face registered a frown. "No denying it," he said, "folks around here is hard on the wildlife."

The shores made for oozy walking. Nevertheless there was much evidence of human visitation: rutted trails dug by four wheel drives among the tupelo, improvised boardwalks of thrown together logs, discarded trot lines, and most pervasive, filth and garbage, much of it malodorous, much of it, in the form of hundreds of aluminum beer cans and plastic bottles, more or less imperishable. Wisner exclaimed angrily about Americans' obsessive need to litter. Quisenberry reflected silently that if the state did acquire the swamp, the public would have greater access to it, and there would be even more of this kind of thing to contend with.

For awhile the three men wandered through the nearby woods. There was no bluff here, and they were gradually forced away from the shoreline as the shallows of the lake extended deeper and deeper into the forest. This was the most extended stand of cypress and tupelo that Quisenberry and Wisner had thus far seen on the tract. Apparently it went on for miles. The boles of the trees were stained a muddy brown to a height of ten or twelve feet, the high water mark of the previous winter's overflow. Even where the earth was dry enough to walk upon, there was not much ground cover, not even dead leaves. Instead there were thousands of crayfish castles, built of mud, and brilliant orange lichens growing on dead driftwood, and the red fallen flowers of trumpet vines that were blooming out of sight above them.

At one point, Murrah exclaimed softly and pointed out across the shallows to a tupelo somewhat larger than its neighbors, its fluid lines collapsing at the base into a mass of slithering roots. "Now that," he whispered, "is one big cottonmouth!"

Quisenberry squinted but said nothing. Wisner, however, spotted the shape at once. It was without a doubt the largest water mocassin he had ever seen. Summoning his courage, he determined to have a somewhat closer look. He began wading cautiously towards it. He had not gone far, however, before he heard the sound of someone strangling behind him. He turned to discover Murrah doubled up with muffled laughter. At a further distance Quisenberry was looking from one to the other, wearing a dry smile, and shaking his head. The cottonmouth, Wisner abruptly realized, was a hoax. He walked a few feet further out into the shallows, far enough to confirm that it was indeed a root, albeit as sinuous and reptilian as a root could get. Returning to dry land, he cursed Murrah heartily, while the unrepentant guide hooted and guffawed.

The rain had begun in earnest again, but there was one more stop. Instead of heading back up the slope when they had reached the highway, Murrah drove the jeep under the bridge and into the forest on the other side. At once the track came to an end, and Murrah announced that they would have to get out and walk again. The damp black earth around them was incisored by deer tracks, so many of them that Quisenberry wondered aloud if the area might not be overpopulated with the animals. Not so, said Murrah; they came through the winters sleek and fat. And it was a fact that even in this spot where most undergrowth had been shaded out, what there was of it didn't look overbrowsed.

Wisner dropped behind, absorbed in the cathedral atmosphere of the place. When he glanced around, he saw Quisenberry and Murrah some distance ahead, their backs to him, looking at something in front of them. Wisner wondered what it could be. At first all he could see was the general, by now familiar, impression of gray and black trunks massed together in the gray-blue light, endlessly repeating themselves in diminishing perspective as though the whole effect were created by mirrors. In this gloom, all color merged and it took him several seconds to realize what he was staring at. Once he did, he could notice nothing else. Before him was the largest cypress he had ever seen, or could ever imagine seeing. It dwarfed all those trees around it which he had been thinking were so large.

It was also, he began to realize, the oddest-looking cypress tree he had ever seen, not because it outdid the normally extravagant tapering, the sometimes grotesque contortions, of that habitually eccentric species, but because it rejected all of that. It was the most matter-of-fact tree in the world, a tree such as a child might draw. Its enormous girth, twenty-eight feet in circumference and at least nine feet in diameter, rose up straight as a smokestack with no visible diminution at all to a height of more than one hundred feet, at which point it abruptly stopped, the top gone, presumably as a consequence of arboreal blight and/or some long ago wind. When Wisner gazed straight up he saw that one side of the vertical shaft was interrupted, half-way up, by an immense knot, a gouty looking extrusion draped in moss and lichen, commodious enough to seat himself and his two companions for a picnic lunch. At eye level, there were small holes through which he could see that the tree was entirely hollow. Quisenberry, circling around the other side, speculated that the core of the cypress must have rotted before the first loggers came here generations before, which was how this one tree got to be left alone.

The effect of all this monumental agedness was neither grand nor solemn; it was better than that. The tree was not only the sort of tree that a child might draw, but one that a child might imaginatively live in. Wisner felt that he had seen it somewhere before, and then dimly remembered the illustrations in his childhood storybooks—the fortress trees built by sympathetic nature to house truant boys and girls as well as clans of elves and dwarfs.

Quisenberry came up next to him. "What a good tree," he said. "A tree like that must have had bears, racoons, owls, 'possums—you name it—living in it at one time or another. Wouldn't be surprised if some of them are living in it now."

Early in the day, Graham Wisner and Quisenberry had explained to Murrah their ambitions for the Pascagoula tract. At the time Murrah had said nothing, but that evening when they were about to part company he remarked, "I wish you fellahs luck, but to be truthful with you, I don't see any way in the world you're goin' to save this swamp." Wisner kidded him for being a pessimist like Quisenberry, but Quisenberry said nothing.

On the trip back to Jackson he and Wisner were more at ease with each other than they had been on the drive down. There was a comfortable silence in which each pursued his own thoughts. Graham Wisner had enjoyed seeing both the swamp and Herman Murrah again, but now he was recollecting the time four years earlier when he had first known them. Quisenberry, however, was reliving everything he had seen and heard that day, the swallow-tailed kite, the truncated cypress tree, the cutoff and the oxbow lakes, Murrah's running commentary. He was not the sort of person to commit himself impulsively to anyone or anything, but he was committed now to the idea that the Pascagoula was worth saving. There was no doubt that it was the most impressive natural area left in the state. Murrah was probably right about the near impossibility of rescuing it. All the same, the effort would have to be made.

As he drove through the rainy evening, Quisenberry smiled. For the first time in more than a year he felt sure that he had chosen the right profession for himself.

CHAPTER VIII

Quisenberry's Road Show

IT WAS FORTUNATE that Quisenberry discovered this sense of mission when he did, since it was all that kept him going during some of the more gloomy and exhausting hours of the following fall and winter. While Morine dickered unsuccessfully with Pascagoula Hardwood Company, and Avery Wood and the Heritage Committee strove to devise a means to buy the swamp if its owners could be persuaded to sell, Quisenberry was assigned one of the most challenging aspects of the Pascagoula project. It would be his task, Wood told him, to convince the state's citizens that the swamp must be saved—with their tax money.

Wood often had occasion to congratulate himself for "discovering" Quisenberry, the perfect aide-de-camp. The young man was intelligent, hard working, willing to follow instructions, and—most important from Wood's point of view—methodical. All sorts of tiresome details concerning the commission and the Heritage Committee could be turned over to Quisenberry with the assurance that they would be efficiently disposed of. Yet although Wood was grateful for Quisenberry's self-effacing personality, he fretted about it too. "I never did run into anyone in my life that had more stronger Christian feelings than Bill," he would exclaim, "but at the same time I never run into anybody that thought less of himself." It did not occur to him to relate the one condition to the other. Even more, however, he was troubled by Quisenberry's reticence. "I tried to break down walls between us, but I always felt that he didn't trust me as far as I trusted him."

Wood wanted very much to be loved and admired, by the world in general and his staff in particular. With his subordinates he was bluff and hearty, insisting that they call him by his first name and that they be as candid with him as he was with them. But he would often lose patience, especially when he was confronted with the petty but sometimes necessary rules that accompany all administrative processes. Dave Morine remembers observing Wood as he chaired a meeting of game wardens who had come in from all over the state. Wood was trying to clarify some fairly cut-and-dried regulation about how mileage was to be recorded for state-owned vehicles. When he opened the floor to questions from his audience, one warden after another began asking about various exceptions to the rule. As this what-if-this-happens? routine went on and on, Wood became visibly exasperated. Finally he broke in on one questioner: "Look," he said, "this here regulation is just like a little bitty fishbone. It ain't very important unless you let it get stuck in your throat. Then you're in a heap of trouble. My advice is, don't get caught. Now let's move on." He then introduced the next subject on the agenda, leaving some of the wardens to find out the answers to their questions on their own.

Wood often complained loudly, sometimes with good reason, that the personnel in the commission lacked initiative; and when he talked with them he was apt to let loose streaks of blue language by way of emphasis, without paying much heed to the age or sex of his listeners. To some extent, this last was a deliberate stratagem, part of his campaign to "break down walls" and loosen people up. But it was not always successful. Some of his subordinates concluded that he was erratic, unsuited to administrative work, and, most damning of all, "common." Even now there are elderly female employees of the Game and Fish Commission who flee the room at mention of his name. The majority view is more generous, and some of his staff remember his reign as a lost golden age. But even his admirers acknowledge that Wood was better as an idea man than an administrator, and that sometimes he came on a bit strong. As for Quisenberry, he has little to say about his relations with Wood, but he too admits that his boss occasionally alienated members of the staff by roaring when he should have purred. In general, however, he concludes that Wood was "the kind of man who made things happen," and that when he departed the agency he left "many more pluses than minuses behind."

Quisenberry must nevertheless have found it a strain to work under Wood, and one can understand Wood's frustration in trying unsuccessfully to reach out to him. To his reserved and diffident lieutenant, Wood's robust overtures must have seemed like verbal bear hugs; all the joshing and kibitzing, the sudden changes of mood, were not the sort of behavior with which he could relate. Quisenberry tried valiantly to obey that rule that one should judge not, for fear of being judged, but the fact remained that Wood's drinking, smoking, profanity, and generally irregular lifestyle did not accord with his own Baptist view of how one ought to live. In short, these two essentially decent and dedicated men were poles apart, and it was a measure of the difference between them that Bill Quisenberry accepted this difference as unbridgeable and Avery Wood did not.

Ironically, Quisenberry acted as self-assured as Wood wanted him to be only on the rare occasions when they were openly opposed. Dave Morine recalls a day when the three of them were driving along the expressway on their way to an appointment, with Wood at the wheel, doing his usual ninety miles an hour, talking all the while. Morine was undisturbed; "after all, it was an official car and Avery Wood was a good driver." Quisenberry, on the other hand, was "hating every minute more than the last." Finally he announced that either Wood must stop the car at once and let him take over or else he must stop it and let him out; he would find his way back to town as best he could. Completely flummoxed by this outburst, Wood pulled over to the shoulder and surrendered the driver's seat to Quisenberry without argument, after which the journey was resumed at a modest 50 mph.

Rebellion, however, was hardly Quisenberry's usual style. When Wood asked him to recruit public support for the Pascagoula project, it did not occur to him to argue that he might not be the right man for the job, or that countless hours of unpaid overtime would obviously be involved. In a sense, he had already begun the assignment in mid-August, a week after the expedition with Wisner. This was when he returned to the swamp with Melvin Tingle, the commission's public relations man, to make a twenty-minute film of it. Before its debut at the Wildlife Heritage Committee meeting, Wood had ordered a considerable amount of editing. The film had sufficient footage of some splendid scenery, but there had not been enough time to get many shots of recreational activities or wildlife, which Wood, in one of his more pragmatic moods, realized would be the main selling points of the swamp. After all, the governor liked to fish, and everybody else in Mississippi like to fish, and everybody everywhere liked to look at wild birds and animals. He told Tingle and Quisenberry to raid the commission's film library for appropriate footage. It wasn't cheating, he assured them, since the scenes they were looking for could have been shot in the Pascagoula Swamp even if they weren't. In due course, the revisions were completed, the Pascagoula now populated by smiling fishermen and wading whitetail deer from every part of the state.

Quisenberry was the first to admit that, except for availability and dedication, he had few qualifications for the job Wood had assigned him. Selling of any kind usually requires an extroverted temperament which Quisenberry manifestly did not have. During the next several months there were many occasions when he would ask himself why he had ever gotten into the swamp-saving business in the first place.

Like many other people in this story, Quisenberry had not guessed that he was destined for this line of work when he was growing up. He had spent his childhood and adolescence in a suburb outside of Jackson, a quiet, dutiful son much overshadowed by a younger brother whom everyone, including Quisenberry, considered more brilliant and talented than himself. Even now, when he was turning thirty-three, he lacked the self-confidence that characterized men like Wood and Morine.

His early exposure to wildlife and ecology consisted mostly of watching television specials about rounding up elk or darting rhinos. He certainly never thought of wildlife management as a career. While he was an undergraduate at Mississippi College, Quisenberry avoided science courses, including biology, whenever he could. His conversion came about during a restless summer while he was still "piddling around," not knowing what he wanted to do with his life. He took a job as a seasonal park ranger in Rocky Mountain National Park, and there discovered that he had "an affinity" for wilderness, "all that unspoiled space" in which to be left alone. When he came home he switched his major to biology, which meant two years of additional undergraduate work. Afterwards, though he now had at least a general idea of a professional field, he found himself in the occupational limbo familiar to millions of young people during the Vietnam years. Late in 1966, at the suggestion of one of his former professors, he applied to the Mississippi Game and Fish Commission for a job and was quickly hired. After two years of collecting statistics on game harvests in the state, he went back to college during a leave of absence and took a degree in wildlife ecology. But by this time he was seriously thinking of leaving the commission.

"I was never much interested in game management *per se*," Quisenberry explains. "I didn't want money all that much—anybody who's interested in money isn't in my field—but I did want a challenge. I wasn't getting any satisfaction from putting pretty bands on mourning doves; and I never cared too much about going through deer guts looking for parasites. Or listening to deer hunters tell their stories. Of course," he adds, "I support hunting. It's what puts bread on my table and keeps the game species going. But my interest was always more generalized. You know, like the Pascagoula. It's the whole thing that interests me. Not just recreation, but the thing itself."

The Heritage Committee as a means, and the Pascagoula as an end, had entered his life just when he had made up his mind to find a new job. After that, he forgot that he had ever meant to leave. Though unlike Wood or Morine in every outward respect, Quisenberry shared with them the notion that his life ought to serve some perceivably useful purpose. Until 1974, however, there had been no cause, no manifestation of "the whole thing," to which he could commit himself. His personal discovery of the Pascagoula had now resolved that problem.

During those summer days in the swamp, first with Wisner, then with Melvin Tingle, he had conceived an affection for it that was more personal than Morine's or Woods's obsession with the place. To them it was the most important and challenging of all possible projects. To him, it was "the thing itself" that mattered. This least likely of champions, uncombative, unexpectant of winning, accepted the rescue of the vast swamp as a personal crusade. None of which lessened his dismay when Avery Wood told him to convince the people of the state that the Pascagoula must be saved, no matter what the cost.

Dave Morine recalls Quisenberry during those days. "He was our resident Cassandra. Avery and the others on the committee were upbeat by nature. Me too, I guess, although there were times when I figured two or three years of my life were going down the drain. But Bill—he would shake his head and say it couldn't be done. Then he'd go right on doing what couldn't be done anyway."

Quisenberry's assignment comprised almost all the activities imaginable for which he considered himself unsuited. He liked staying put; the idea of being an itinerant salesman, always on the road, repelled him. He was reserved in the presence of strangers, preferring to back up more outgoing types like Wood and Morine than to deal with them on his own. He had a positive dread of public speaking and was convinced he wasn't good at it. (He still swears that it was the film that did the selling, not his speeches.) He disliked having to drive long distances, often from one end of the state to the other; and because he was so cautious behind the wheel it took him a long time to get where he was going. Worst of all, familiarity did not decrease his fear of flying, especially in the small, vibrating planes owned by the state; yet often his speaking engagements were so tightly scheduled that it was the only possible way to travel.

Even a man better suited to the job would have found it a prodigious undertaking. Between November, 1974, and May, 1976, Quisenberry added to his regular work load some 450 speaking engagements, an average of one a day including weekends. These appearances, many of which he solicited himself, were scattered randomly across the state and the calendar, whenever groups in Biloxi or Natchez or anywhere in between could fit him into their schedules of meetings. At the same time, Quisenberry was also contacting sports writers and members of the news media. He appeared on numerous television and radio talk shows and helped produce and distribute a public service TV spot advertising the Heritage Committee and its Pascagoula project.

On a typical day he might work in his office until 2:00 or 3:00 PM, then drive one hundred miles or more to a small Mississippi town, take a quick supper at a motel restaurant or hamburger stand, appear at the local schoolhouse or VFW hall in time to set up the projector, deliver his talk and show the film to the group that had invited him, hand out draft resolutions and sample letters that the group could copy and send to its legislators, then drive back to Jackson, arriving home about midnight. Too many successive days and nights like these sadly disrupted his orderly, early-to-bed routine. He was often tired and cranky, and his wife, though "a good sport" as a rule, occasionally lost her patience too. Sometimes the scheduling could get even worse. On one such occasion, Quisenberry began the day by presenting his talk and film for the breakfast meeting of a group in Jackson; then he drove a hundred miles south to Natchez for a noon engagement with the local Lions Club; after that he drove back to the Jackson airport where a state plane was waiting to fly him to Columbus in northeastern Mississippi. He arrived just in time for a meeting with a local hunting and fishing club. When he finally reached his own front door it was 1:00 AM.

The air flights, a torment under the best of circumstances, were occasionally made worse by bad weather. Quisenberry particularly remembers one flight when the plane hit a line of thunderstorms which the pilot could not get around. "The plane was a Cessna 310," he recalls. "It began bouncing around like a jack-in-the-box, with thunder and lightning on all sides. Micky Meeks, the pilot, had been talking about one thing and another when we started out but now he wasn't saying a word. Then I noticed his hands were just glued to the stick and his knuckles were white. If he was scared, I wondered what I was supposed to be! Finally we did break through the storm without much damage. But by then, of course, I'd been airsick two or three times."

Whether because he lost his lunch so often, or because he was more worried and overworked than usual, he lost fifteen pounds and gained an ulcer during the months when his "road show" was most heavily booked.

During this period Quisenberry met with more groups than he had ever supposed existed—Lions and Rotary clubs, Daughters of the American Revolution, a convention of land surveyors, chambers of commerce, the Mississippi Bicentennial Commission, businessmen's associations, the Mississippi Economic Council, an Audubon chapter, innumerable hunting and fishing groups, dozens of garden clubs, even church groups on Sunday mornings. Although the response to his presentations was always enthusiastic, he was uncertain at first whether this enthusiasm would be translated into action. This was not a bread and butter issue, after all, and Mississippians were not especially noted for being environmental activists. But he need not have worried. Before long, some state legislators were reporting to him and Wood that they were receiving more mail urging them to save the Pascagoula than they had ever received on any other single issue. For many of these politicians this outpouring of concern was a revelation. Citizens were normally opposed to increased state spending of any kind, for good reason: the median income of Mississippians was far below the national average; public services were often minimal; and, because of the relatively small population, state taxes were quite high. Yet here were thousands of ordinary people, some of them not as strong on grammar as they were on feeling, urging their representatives to spend millions of state dollars on the purchase of a tract of land that only a few years earlier would have been regarded as a wasteland. The message was plain enough. As far as their natural heritage was concerned, the state's citizens were voting in favor of Mississippi-as-it-is. Most heartening of all from the Wildlife Heritage Committee's point of view, much of this mail was coming from the northern and western sectors of the state, from people who had never heard of the Pascagoula Swamp until they listened to Quisenberry's talk and saw his film.

As the publicity campaign gathered momentum, citizen conservation groups joined in to help. One of the first to lend support was the influential Mississippi Wildlife Federation, whose director, Polly Anderson, was one of Quisenberry's strongest backers. Before long, so many offers of assistance were pouring into commission headquarters that Quisenberry could not handle all of them.

Dave Morine would later observe that "the whole operation was an object lesson in how much even one person can accomplish if the will is there." That the will, in this case, was contained in a vessel as determinedly self-effacing as Bill Quisenberry made the achievement all the more impressive.

However, Quisenberry himself took little satisfaction in the growing evidence that his efforts were successful. There was not much time for self-congratulation even if he had been disposed to anything so self-indulgent. More important, a sense of dread was growing in him. "Here I was, telling all those audiences that we had to have money, lots of money, to buy this swamp—and all the while there was no certainty that we *could* buy it. In fact, as the months went on and public support grew stronger, the likelihood of us buying it got dimmer and dimmer. I figured that if we didn't succeed, I'd be run out of the state. And all that work gone for nothing! I used to have nightmares. Really. Nightmares."

By the beginning of 1975, Quisenberry was not the only one who was deeply worried. Dave Morine was having second thoughts about the project and his own involvement in it. He knew better than anyone else that his negotiations with Pascagoula Hardwood were getting nowhere. If anything, the company's officers were more determined than ever not to sell to the Conservancy or the state. Hynson's December 9 letter to Morine could not have been plainer on that point. He felt, not for the last time, that he had allowed "crazy Avery's" certainty that any obstacle could be overcome to carry him away. He was a professional optimist himself, but he was beginning to conclude that Wood's stop-at-nothing zeal was naive, even perhaps harmful to the Conservancy's aims and his own reputation. The man's assurance was all too catching. "Here was Quisenberry committing public relations miracles out in the sticks, and the Heritage Committee rarin' and ready to go; even the committee's politicians, shrewd, cautious people, were sold on the idea of introducing an appropriations bill at the next legislative session." Indeed, Morine's earlier wish that committee members should become more sophisticated in their attitude towards land acquisition had been realized only too well. Now they were in no mood to settle for second best.

The problem was that Wood's sense of mission would have no effect on decisions made in that elegant marble board room in Laurel, where the state had now begun to assume the character of an ardent but unwanted suitor who would not take no for an answer. Pascagoula Hardwood's directors and stockholders, many of the latter still unaware of Morine's efforts to make a deal with the company, were reading about Quisenberry's public appearances in their local papers and were wondering what was going on.

Morine now had to admit that the momentum behind the Pascagoula project had gotten out of his control. If all these growing expectations were disappointed, which seemed likely, his reputation and the Nature Conservancy's credibility were bound to suffer. It was possible that everything he had hoped to accomplish in Mississippi would be jeopardized.

Morine attended the Heritage Committee meeting of January 16, 1975, much preoccupied by these concerns and determined to say something about them. Prior to the meeting, Avery Wood had been working with Charles Deaton, the influential member from the state House of Representatives, to decide how best to convince the legislature to find money to purchase the swamp, and this was the main topic on the agenda.

Morine had arranged to be asked to speak first. "Gentlemen," he began, "I know that ever since last summer, the Pascagoula has been the property we've most wanted to acquire. But we should be careful about putting all our eggs in one basket. We should be giving our attention to other projects in the state as well. Now that some of the Game and Fish Commission's frozen funds have been transferred to this committee, several hundred thousand dollars, we ought to put that money to work. We should be looking at some other areas like the Pearl River Basin. We don't want to get tied down to a single objective, especially since we aren't sure that the Pascagoula Hardwood Company will sell its land." He cleared his throat. "The fact is, gentlemen, that it is possible we might not be able to acquire that land after all."

There was complete silence for several seconds. Morine was uncomfortably aware that everyone was looking at him "funny." Then Coach John Vaught leaned forward, gave Morine a long stare as though wondering whether he ought to be on the team or not, and said, "Son, I reckon you just don't know how we work in Mississippi. Down here, son, we go for the touchdown on every play." At this, everyone else at the table exchanged satisfied smiles and nods. Bill Allen, the chairman, said, "I'll second that. Now let's get down to business." Morine sat down.

During the rest of the meeting, the proposed funding bill was the main subject of discussion. Deaton argued persuasively that the legislature would be more likely to go along with the proposal if the money came from a general obligation bond issue rather than from the General Fund, and this approach was voted favorably. As for the amount of money that would be needed, the only indication of the value of the Pascagoula tract was the amount that Masonite had previously bid for an exchange of shares, namely, $15 million. It was agreed that this was the sum that the state must come up with.

Avery Wood left the meeting grinning from ear to ear; everyone else was looking pleased about what had been accomplished too. Everyone, that is, except Morine. He shook his head and nervously touched the pocket which contained Hynson's rejecting letter. He had originally meant to read it to the committee; but then the momentum had caught him up again and he had decided he had better not.

CHAPTER IX

The Legislative Battle

IN JANUARY, 1975, House Bill 914, authorizing $15 million for the purchase of the Pascagoula tract, began its hazardous journey through the Mississippi legislature. Wood had decided that the bill should be introduced into the House first, contrary to his usual practice. "Most times when I had a bill ready, I figured it was easier to start out convincing 52 senators before I took on 122 representatives. But this time, with Charlie Deaton sponsoring the bill in the House Appropriations Committee, where it would go first, I knew we'd get some good momentum going; whereas in the Senate I realized there was going to be some special problems." Deaton and Senator Donald Strider, the two Heritage Committee members who would organize support for the bill in the House and Senate respectively, agreed with Wood's plan for the exactly opposite reason: they felt that the House would be the more difficult battleground and might as well be tackled first.

In the unfolding history of the Pascagoula project, Deaton's role was now crucial. He was acting chairman of the House Appropriations Committee and generally regarded by his fellow legislators as an authority on financial issues. In a more general way, he was regarded as a "comer," a man to be reckoned with in the House. Fate had been particularly generous in equipping him for the career he had chosen. He was physically impressive—tall, with Stewart Granger good looks, pale blue eyes, wavy silvering hair, a large smile and deep voice. He projected self-assurance without seeming arrogant, was courtly with women, confidential with men. Even in a large group he could introduce a newcomer to everyone in sight without stumbling at a single name. Urbane one moment, he could be folksy the next, slapping backs and telling jokes appropriate to the company. He was shrewdly intelligent, careful not to stick his political neck out too far, but more capable than most politicians of taking a long view when it was required, seeing beyond the parochial interests of the Delta county he represented.

Deaton had committed himself to state ownership of the Pascagoula because he believed the project would compel Mississippi to reconsider its current policy of neglect regarding recreational lands. He had quickly grasped the significance of Wood's idea for a Heritage Committee and had been largely responsible for the passage of the bill creating it. He had even taken the trouble to understand the Nature Conservancy's concept of ecological inventory and had listened attentively to Morine's warning about uncontrolled industrial growth. Moreover, he recognized that the issue of environmental protection could be a means, in Wood's phrase, of "turning the state around." If Mississippi could take the lead in formulating enlightened environmental legislation, there was no reason to doubt that it could take the lead in other areas as well.

Wood and Deaton had grown up together on Greenwood's East Market Street, one of the town's poorer neighborhoods. In those days the two boys saw a lot of each other and got along well. Since then, however, their relationship had become more complex, at least from Wood's point of view. He continues to admire Deaton, "the most honorable politician in the state," and acknowledges his invaluable support in getting various environmental bills through the House. But he is sometimes apt to qualify this praise. "Charlie's only trouble is that he's done forget he comes from East Market Street," Wood says. "He's gone over to the establishment. He's got no more business being part of the establishment than I do. I know his honor and integrity; I'd go to the wall for him. It's just that I think he'd be the living end in politics if he'd only come out and be himself; if he'd come back to East Market Street, you know? He wouldn't need nobody but Charlie Deaton then." According to Avery Wood, this equivocal view derives from the two men's public roles. Wood, the governor's appointee, continually fretted over the legislature's control of Game and Fish Commission's funds. Deaton, he says, was too concerned with preserving and expanding legislative powers—in spite of the fact that Deaton had helped bring into being the Heritage Committee, an agency remarkable for its autonomy.

In fact, Wood's mixed feelings about Deaton spring largely from a more personal source: "My biggest problem is suaveness, the lack of it," he admits, not without some satisfaction. "Maybe I go off the deep end sometimes; but I tell you, give me a man who goes off the deep end to one who doesn't anytime. I'll take a lie detector test every twenty-four hours, and I got nothing to hide. I challenge any suave and cool politician to do the same." Wood adds, "You give me five Dave Morines in the House and Senate and one of me in the House and Senate, and there wouldn't be nothing we was last at—except stealing." Wood knows perfectly well that Morine is usually as suave and cool as any politician; but that does not bother him because Morine works for a nonprofit organization and is willing, and able, to take risks. Besides, he comes from New England—not, as Deaton does, from Wood's own neighborhood. Wood's impatience with the niceties of diplomacy and compromise is genuine ("great minds discuss ideas"), but he must occasionally wonder how far he might have gone—as far as Deaton, perhaps—if he had had more "suaveness."

It is unlikely that Charles Deaton envies Wood his outspoken temperament. He would point out, fairly enough, that accommodation is essential to the political process and that, in any case, he has taken risks when the issue warranted it. But he is not indifferent to his old friend's ambivalent feelings concerning him. He thinks highly of Wood, he says—but only after first asking what Wood has said of him.

If these undercurrents of feeling are of any interest it is because of the influence they did not have on the two men's professional relationship. In practice, Deaton's political skills and Wood's brash idealism were both essential, and the pair worked effectively as a team. Both knew that at this point it was the political art of the possible that counted most. Deaton believed that by the time a bill came to the House floor, its fate should already be settled. Not taking risks was now a necessary strategy. "Tell me when you're ready to go," he told Wood, "and I'll take it from there. But make damn sure you're really ready." Being ready, in this case, meant preparing data on the Pascagoula, on Mississippi's recreational needs, on the economic importance of the state's outdoor recreation industry. It meant keeping track of the public's response to Quisenberry's efforts to sell the appropriations bill. It also meant writing the bill itself, and for this purpose Deaton arranged that one of the House's specialists in drafting legislation, Bud Thigpen, should lend his services to Wood, Morine, and Quisenberry. Finally, it meant defusing as much potential legislative opposition as possible before the bill ever reached the floor.

On that last count, Wood made numerous trips to the capitol. By this time he had developed a taboo relating to that imposing building: he must never enter through its huge main doors; if he did, the mission that had brought him there would surely fail. As a result, his familiar figure could be seen time after time skirting the wide entrance stairway, hurrying towards the less imposing doorway underneath. Inside, he cornered legislators at their desks or in the corridors, barraging them with data about how H.B. 914 would benefit their constituents, why it was needed, how the state could afford the cost of purchase, why it was necessary to raise the money without a previous commitment on the part of Pascagoula Hardwood.

A particular source of concern was the opposition of two large hunting clubs which, between them, leased most of the Pascagoula tract for their private use. State ownership of the land would inevitably preclude private access and would throw the area open to the public. Members of the clubs had begun a letter-writing campaign of their own and were putting considerable pressure on their representatives. It required the combined effort of Deaton, Wood, and Quisenberry to convince these legislators to resist.

Another far more influential lobby also had to be dealt with. Private timber companies comprised one of Mississippi's most economically important industries, and their political influence was very great. They were traditionally unfriendly to the idea of state ownership of wildlands, partly because they did not wish to compete with the state for acquisition of available tracts, partly because they feared that state-owned lands would be removed from timber production. Their past opposition was one of the chief reasons why Mississippi possessed so few public recreational areas. Wood and Quisenberry decided "to beard the lion in his den." They arranged for the state forester, Billy Gaddis, to set up a meeting with representatives of all the major timber companies operating in the state. Undoubtedly, as least some of those present were aware that the governor had intervened when International Paper Company had shown some interest in Pascagoula Hardwood. Whether because of Waller's evident bias in favor of state ownership of the swamp, or because of the impact of Wood's speech and Quisenberry's film, the atmosphere at the meeting was friendly enough. And in the forthcoming legislative process, the timber industry offered no perceivable opposition to H.B. 914.

Late in January, 1975, Wood went once again to Deaton's office and told him he was as ready as he ever would be. Deaton immediately placed the bill on the calendar for consideration by the House Appropriations Committee. Under his sponsorship, it was approved and ready for debate on the House floor. There were several delays during which the bill was kept in a holding pattern, and it was not until February 27 that it was finally introduced. Deaton had done his work well. There was little outright opposition to the bill and it passed easily—99 to 14. However, what should have been an occasion for rejoicing became instead another crisis. During the last minutes of the debate that preceded the passage of H.B. 914, an amendment had been unexpectedly introduced by one of the legislators requiring that most of the Pascagoula tract, when it became the property of the state, would be managed by the State Forestry Commission as a commercial timber resource. Deaton, reluctant to jeopardize the $15 million appropriation by challenging the amendment, allowed it to pass.

Wood and Quisenberry were not the only ones troubled by this development. Both Graham Wisner and his older brother, Ellis, had been following the progress of the bill with considerable interest. Ellis Wisner, as the family's business manager, had mixed feelings about the state's, and the Conservancy's, ambition for the swamp. He was not indifferent to Graham's desire to see the Pascagoula preserved. But his first responsibility was to his family and its financial interests, and he was not at all sure that his brother's hopes and his own obligations could be reconciled. For the time being, he was prepared to keep an open mind. However, word of the amendment to House Bill 914 changed all this. What was the point of giving the state any special consideration if its plans for the tract were similar to those of Masonite or International Paper? He advised Wood that he and his family would do all they could to oppose the bill in the Senate if the amendment were allowed to stand.

With this threat ringing in his ears, Wood headed once again for Deaton's office. Within hours both men were buttonholing legislators in the halls and the House chamber, frantically trying to convince them that the amendment had to be repealed. Finally, after several days of intensive lobbying, the offending provision was brought back to the floor and voted down.

The Wisners were not the only ones paying close attention to the fate of H.B. 914. The day after the House approved the appropriations bill, the president of Pascagoula Hardwood, Bob Hynson, called Quisenberry from Laurel and arranged to meet him the next morning, March 1 at the River Hills Tennis Club in Jackson. Quisenberry spent a sleepless night wondering if Hynson and the other officers of Pascagoula Hardwood Company were planning to launch their own attack against the bill.

As matters turned out, the meeting proved less traumatic than he had feared. If anything, it seemed to be Hynson who was troubled. For the first time he was beginning to take the state seriously. More particularly, he was concerned that the legislature might use its authority to condemn the Pascagoula tract, thereby guaranteeing its purchase by the state. Was there a possibility that such a step was being considered? Cautiously, Quisenberry acknowledged that the state did indeed have the power of condemnation but that, thus far, the option was not being considered. In fact, Quisenberry was convinced that the legislature would never consider such a measure, though he knew that Avery Wood was nurturing that option as a recourse if all else failed. In any case, if Hynson was less than totally reassured, Quisenberry reflected, that was perhaps just as well. Hynson questioned Quisenberry closely about the appropriation bill's chances in the Senate; and as the two men parted company, he asserted strongly—but not as strongly as Quisenberry had feared—that the directors of Pascagoula Hardwood would not be induced to sell the property just because the state appropriated money for that purpose.

The senate battle was now begun. Right at the outset, a serious problem presented itself. In the Senate, as in the House, two different committees, the Appropriations and the Ways and Means (Finance) committees, dealt with financial legislation. In the ordinary course of things, House Bill 914, having been referred to the House Appropriations Committee, would have been sent to its Senate counterpart. This was an eventuality that Avery Wood wanted desperately to avoid, notwithstanding the fact that Senator Strider, a member of the Heritage Committee and a staunch supporter of the bill, was also a member of Appropriations. Strider's advocacy could not match the influence of the Appropriations Committee chairman, Senator Bill Burgin, whom Wood regarded as an implacable foe of the measure. Even less engaged observers considered it likely that if the bill went to Burgin's committee it would die there. Burgin was one of Waller's most relentless political enemies and any legislation that the governor supported was likely to earn his opposition. (Reputedly, the vendetta began when Burgin urged the director of the State Welfare Department to hire one of his supporters, a not uncommon practice. In this case, however, the man was so manifestly unqualified that the director refused, and Waller backed him up. Burgin was so furious that he would not allow the customary photo of the new governor to be hung in the Appropriations Committee room.) Wood was also convinced that Burgin had never forgiven him his appointment as director of the Game and Fish Commission.

The previous director had been Burgin's close personal friend and the senator had done all that he could to keep him in his post when Waller came to office. "From the beginning," Wood claims, "Burgin hated my guts. As far as he was concerned I couldn't ever do nothing right." Quisenberry's view is more impartial. He acknowledges Burgin's dislike of Waller and Wood but suggests that more objective considerations were possibly at work: "Senator Burgin was usually an ally of the Game and Fish Commission; but he gave low priority to the whole idea of land acquisition for recreation. He just didn't think it was a worthwhile way to spend the taxpayers' money."

Whatever Burgin's motives at the time, the bill's partisans recognized that the senator would kill it if he could. It was imperative that it should not fall into his hands. Wood appealed to the lieutenant governor, William Winter, to help him out. As presiding officer of the Senate, it was Winter's prerogative to refer bills to appropriate committees for consideration. Senator Strider had already tried to persuade Winter to send H.B. 914 to the Senate Game and Fish Committee, which he chaired, but without success. Wood had more luck. He described the importance of the bill, outlined the problem, and persuaded the lieutenant governor to send it to the Senate Finance Committee instead of Appropriations.

Wood realized that in averting a known danger, he was sailing into uncharted seas. The chairman of Finance, Senator Ellis Bodron, was one of the most powerful men in the Senate, but also, as far as this bill was concerned, an unknown quantity. Senator "Son" Rhodes, a Heritage Committee member and supporter of the bill, was also a member of the Finance Committee and on good terms with Bodron. Useful as this connection was, Wood was not convinced that it would be enough to guarantee the bill's survival. When he learned that Bodron had scheduled H.B. 914 to be brought before the committee on March 6, he decided to call Dave Morine to speak in support of the bill. This was a calculated risk. Although Morine had made himself liked and respected by the legislative members of the Heritage Committee and assorted other politicians, most of the senators at the Finance hearing, including

Bodron, would not know him. Wood was not at all sure how they would react to an outsider, especially one with an extravagantly Bostonian accent and a Brooks Brothers style.

Of the many episodes that comprise the story of the Pascagoula project, none is more vividly fixed in Morine's recollection than this committee hearing. On the appointed day, he and Wood sat outside the meeting room for more than an hour, waiting to be called in. "Avery was pacing back and forth, nervous as a cat, swearing under his breath, chain-smoking as usual. Every time a senator passed by on his way into the conference room, Avery would try to be polite to him, but you could tell the senators didn't want to be bothered. I felt embarrassed. I was wondering what the hell I'd got myself into." Finally they were asked to enter.

It was at once evident that most of the legislators present felt that the meeting was, for all practical purposes, already over. Senator Bodron was blind, but he ran the committee with remarkable efficiency, relying on his memory and the briefing he received before each meeting to introduce items on the agenda in their correct order, recite facts and figures, and control discussion. A senator sitting next to him, Martin Smith, recognized speakers, but Bodron knew where they sat and faced them when they spoke.

By the time that Wood, Morine, and H.B. 914 had become the next item of business, the meeting was about to run overtime. Most of the committee members were leaning back in their chairs, reading newspapers or talking to one another. Wood hurriedly introduced Morine, who began to deliver his prepared statement. He had not gotten very far before Bodron interrupted, apologetic but firm: "Thank you for taking the trouble to come down here, Mr. Morine," he said. "I wish we could give you more time, but as you see, we've gotten behind schedule. You may rest assured that we will give your bill every consideration . . ."

Morine was suddenly angry. "Most of these guys hadn't even put down their newspapers when we came in. They weren't listening to me; they weren't even going to consider the bill. All they wanted was for me to say hello and get out. I was really pissed. I'd become as whacky as

Avery by this time. I don't know what came over me. Suddenly I yelled,
'Senator Bodron, members of the committee, you people are throwing
away your birthright!' Well, at that, people lowered their newspapers
and took the cigars out of their mouths, and Senator Bodron started
rapping his gavel and saying "Mr. Morine, I'm afraid we don't have
time . . .' But I was too wound up now. 'Forget the Pascagoula tract for
the moment,' I said. 'You got the bill, you can read it for yourselves.
What I'm talking about now is the preservation of a way of life. People
in Mississippi have always been close to their land, but now all that's
changing. They're going to be as homogenized as the rest of the country
unless you do something about it. I'm from Boston, as you can
probably tell, and I've seen all the things I lived with as a boy destroyed.
Unless you take a stand, the way of life you people take for granted is
going to be lost forever. What we're talking about here is not the
preservation of a swamp but the preservation of a way of life!' "

There was some confusion in the room as Morine, angry at everyone,
aghast at his own audacity, headed for the door. He was about to open
it when he heard one of the senators addressing Senator Bodron: "Mr.
Chairman, if you don't mind, there are some questions I'd like to ask
Mr. Morine, I want to hear more of what he has to say." There was a
general murmur of support for this sentiment. Morine came back to his
chair. Senator Bodron's sunglasses stared sightlessly at him. "Very well,
Mr. Morine," he said, "we really don't have time today, but if you will
tell us your schedule, we'll set up another meeting." Although Morine's
schedule was particularly crowded at this time, he assured Bodron that
he would make himself available whenever the committee wished to see
him. The date of March 12 was agreed upon, and the meeting was over.
Outside, Morine discovered that he was soaked with perspiration.
"Avery was beaming," Morine recalls, "but the s.o.b. didn't even say,
'Nice job!' He just assumed that was the way you were supposed to act."

Two days before this second meeting, Quisenberry, with the help of
National Guard helicopters and commission boats, provided the mem-
bers of a Finance subcommittee with a tour of the Pascagoula Swamp.
Everyone seemed to enjoy himself except Quisenberry, who was airsick

once again. This tour, and accounts of Morine's performance, attracted considerable attention, so that virtually all the members of the Finance Committee showed up for the closed hearing. This time there were no raised newspapers in view and many of the senators had done their homework on the bill. At the beginning of the meeting, Bodron insisted that Quisenberry show the Pascagoula film, though he could not see it himself. Afterwards, the questions began. "Those sons-of-a-gun asked me every question in the world," says Morine, "One of the senators, Fred Rogers, was a timberman, and under his direction the committee had really done its homework. It was the most intense grilling I'd ever been through: 'How many acres were involved?' 'How much timber?' 'How would the appropriation be paid back?' 'How would the area be used?' 'What was in it for the Nature Conservancy?' 'Why should the state put up money without a commitment from Pascagoula Hardwood?' During that session I completely reversed my opinion of Mississippi politicians."

Morine was in his element. There was no emotion now, just facts and figures. "I knew what I was supposed to know. I could sense it was going well. Besides," he explains, "I was wearing my negotiating undies." This garment was a pair of "lucky" blue shorts which Morine always wore at meetings of more than usual importance. It had not struck him as at all inconsistent that, while thus attired and accompanying Quisenberry and Wood to the present meeting, he had teased the latter for his superstitious refusal to enter the capitol through the main entrance.

After three hours, the session came to an end. This time as Morine headed for the door, one of the senators remarked aloud that he had never witnessed a more organized and effective presentation. "What the hell," says Morine; "naturally I felt good!"

During this meeting many of the legislators began to grasp for the first time the important role that Morine would play in the impending negotiations with Pascagoula Hardwood. The committee decided it would be a good idea to check up on both him and the Conservancy. He was asked to supply testimonials from other states assuring them that the Conservancy was a reliable organization. Morine lost no time in "cashing in chips" with officials in Georgia, South Carolina, and other states whom he had helped. Within days, the committee was receiving letters of recommendation concerning the sterling attributes of the Conservancy.

Meanwhile, Avery Wood was cashing in some chips of his own. During that March he virtually lived in the Senate, cornering every legislator he could. He was too aggressively earnest, too dogmatic, to make an ideal lobbyist. Nevertheless, his position as director of one of the state's most popular and visible agencies allowed him some leverage. There were numerous, albeit modest, ways that the commission could help a politician win friends and influence voters—arranging for his photo to appear in the county newspaper as the local lake was stocked with fish, hiring a hometown boy as a game warden, releasing wild turkeys on the plantation of an important campaign contributor. These past and future favors added up, and Wood did not hesitate to remind legislators of them now. He kept track of Quisenberry's crowded schedule of speaking engagements and whenever possible latched on to a senator just as his constituents were sending in a flurry of mail supporting the appropriations bill.

Even so, Wood had his work cut out for him. A number of legislators had difficulty readjusting their priorities, even temporarily, from industrial development to preservation. Others were troubled that neither Wood nor Morine could guarantee that the owners of the Pascagoula tract would be willing to sell their property. And finally, Burgin was not the only politician with a grudge against the strong-willed, sometimes stubborn governor and his administrators. They listened to Wood, but many of them would not commit themselves.

In the rare moments spent in his office, Wood fumed and fidgeted. His blackboard was now covered with tallies of votes already promised and those still uncertain. As usual, he stalked back and forth between it and the window through which he stared at the capitol dome with more than usual intensity. To Quisenberry or Morine or whoever else happened by, he would mutter that he was going to ask all the duck hunters in the state to show up at the capitol on the day H.B. 914 reached the Senate floor, armed with guns and duck calls and prepared to initiate a thunderous quacking as the vote began. As for Burgin and any other opponents of the bill, he would "take out a contract on them" if the bill failed to pass.

By March 19, the last day of the legislative session, Wood was reasonably confident that House Bill 914 had the necessary votes if it ever reached the floor. The great question now was whether the Senate would have a chance to vote on it. The bill was trapped in the usual last minute crush of bills whose sponsors were trying to beat the midnight deadline. On this final day, the session was devoted to fiscal matters, and custom usually required that legislation emanating from Burgin's Appropriations Committee should take precedence over that sponsored by Bodron's Finance Committee. In practice, however, the omnibus bill that was annually sponsored by Appropriations contained budgeting provisions for state agencies that were dependent on the passage of certain Finance Committee bills. Thus, Burgin found it necessary to prearrange with Bodron the order in which bills would be introduced, and the two men agreed between them on an hour when the podium would be yielded to Bodron.

Some legislators speculate that on this occasion H.B. 914 was caught in "a Mexican stand-off" with another bill which Burgin wanted to see passed. According to this scenario, Bodron agreed not to bring up 914 until Burgin had gotten his own pet bill through the Senate. Burgin, already aware of the order in which Appropriations bills were listed on the calendar, was counting on the fact that his favored bill would not be introduced until late in the evening. Thus, Bodron would have little time in which to deal with his own crowded calendar of Finance bills; H.B. 914 would never have a chance to be brought to a vote, and would die by default. Some such plan would inevitably appeal to Burgin since, as Senator Strider remarks, "he didn't want to make an open fight over the bill because so many of us supported it and he knew he'd lose a lot of friends."

Meantime, Senator Bodron had promised Wood that H.B. 914 would be brought up, and with that assurance Wood and Quisenberry had left the matter to him. Now, however, Wood learned to his dismay that the Rules Committee, which determined the order in which legislation was to be introduced, had placed his bill far down on the Finance calendar. Thus, if it reached the floor at all, it would not be until late in the evening. For Wood and Quisenberry the tension was almost unbearable. Until now they had been able to feel that the legislation was at least theirs to influence, if not control. Now, however, there was nothing further they could do except wait.

That evening after dinner, Quisenberry stationed himself in the visitors' gallery overlooking the ornate Senate chamber. Avery Wood and Bill Allen climbed the rotunda stairs to the encircling balcony and joined Waller in the governor's office. The three men settled down to listen, through the speaker system, to the last hours of the Senate session. Eight o'clock, nine o'clock, nine-thirty passed, while Burgin and his Appropriations bills still held the floor, monopolizing debate. Wood began to pace the floor. In the Senate gallery, Quisenberry's face, always a bit worried-looking, became a study in unalloyed gloom.

Not until ten o'clock did Burgin yield his place to Bodron, and the debate of Finance bills began. Bodron moved as expeditiously as possible; bill after bill was introduced, debated, passed or voted down, but H.B. 914 was still far down the list. Eleven o'clock passed, then eleven-thirty. Waller glanced at his watch, then at his calendar of legislation. "I'm sorry, Avery," he said. "There are still seven or eight bills ahead of yours. I don't see how you can make it."

For once in his life, Wood was a beaten man. It seemed to him that he had never invested himself in anything as much as the passage of this bill. Without it, the Pascagoula was certainly lost, and so, perhaps, was Mississippi's heritage program and the environmental principles it encompassed. The chance to do "one big thing" with the job Waller had handed him—with his life, really—was about to slip away. And nothing about that prospect was as bitter as the thought that he would lose by default. He had had the votes. He had worked hard for them. "Not fair," he muttered, slumping into a chair.

At that moment, 11:35 P.M., the three men were suddenly riveted by Bodron's slow disembodied voice announcing a break with customary procedure. Whether because the plan had been in his mind all along, or because circumstances had compelled him to think of it at the last minute, he now had recourse to an unusual manuever: "Gentlemen," he was saying to the Senate members, "I know there are some good pieces of legislation that we still haven't got to. But with your permission I am going to move that we divert from the calendar and bring House Bill 914 forward for debate." There was considerable risk in this procedure, since the unanimous consent of the Senate was required in order to manipulate the calendar of bills. Bodron, however, counted—rightly— on Burgin's reluctance to oppose the bill openly. His motion carried.

"He's done it! He's done it!" Wood shouted, leaping to his feet, scattering cigarette ashes on the gubernatorial carpet. In the Senate gallery, Quisenberry's boyish face shone like that of an angel on a baroque ceiling. Now that the bill was entered for debate, several senators—Rogers, Rhodes, Strider and others—spoke briefly but effectively in favor of its passage. But Bodron's own comments were the most memorable. "His speech," Wood would later say, "was strong stuff. Here was this blind man who'd never seen the Pascagoula Swamp—yet he had listened to everything that Morine and Quiz and me had said. Now he talked about how in Mississippi it was still possible for even a blind man to enjoy nature, and he described how beautiful the swamp was, just as though he'd seen it, and he said how folks for generations to come would be glad it was preserved."

In fact, however, the agony of suspense was not quite over. Senator Burgin was recognized, and he at once proposed an amendment to the bill that would enable the State Forestry Commission to manage the tract as a commercial timber resource—exactly the same amendment that Wood, Quisenberry, and Deaton had fought so desperately to delete in the House. On this try, however, the motion was soundly defeated, and a few minutes later, House Bill 914 became law. The vote was 52-0. At the end, even Burgin voted for the bill.

At 2:00 A.M., March 20, 1975, Dave Morine's wife, Ruth, was awakened by the ringing phone. She recognized Avery Wood's excited voice at once and nudged her husband awake. When she held the receiver to his ear, the first thing Morine heard was: "Bubba, we done pulled this caper off!"

CHAPTER X

The Four Families

AMONG THE 110 SHAREHOLDERS in Pascagoula Hardwood, there were quite a few besides the Wisners and Bob Hynson who followed the legislative odyssey of H.B. 914 with more than passing interest. The families descended from the Gardiner brothers owned nearly 70 percent of the stock; but the remainder was in the hands of small shareholders who had only a remote connection or none at all with the Gardiner clan. The company, after all, had not originated as a closely held corporation. In the course of three generations, many of the present minority shareholders had acquired stock through inheritance or marriage; some were scarcely aware that it belonged to them. Some had left Mississippi long ago; others had never lived in the state. However, a considerable number of these shareholders still lived in or near Laurel.

Wood and Quisenberry had seen to it that H.B. 914 was widely publicized and supported by the Mississippi news media. Even before the bill was introduced, Quisenberry's publicity campaign urging purchase of the Pascagoula Swamp had been reported in many local papers. He had even brought his road show to Laurel, where he appeared before the local Rotary Club. By the time the bill had cleared the House, quite a few shareholders were understandably wondering what was going on—the more so because the media, in spite of Wood's and Quisenberry's demurrals, seemed to suggest that state acquisition of the swamp would be a foregone conclusion once the bill was passed.

Bob Hynson, as president of the company, began to receive calls and letters from these stockholders. It had not occurred to him to brief them about the state's interest in the swamp. He could reasonably argue that, from the company's point of view, there was nothing to report—no negotiations, no interest, no deal. Indeed, Hynson was apt to be sensitive about this issue of keeping shareholders informed. He was an exceedingly genial man, pleasant to be around, but he shared with Gardiner Green a rather seignorial approach to running the family enterprises. A native of Maryland's Eastern Shore, he married Jane Gardiner Rogers, the granddaughter of George S. Gardiner, in the mid-thirties and moved with her to Laurel in 1941. With the onset of the war, he "fell heir to positions of an executive nature" which he had held ever since. "Mr. Bob," as everyone in Laurel calls him, was a cultivated man, something of a bon vivant, who found the comfortable circumstances in which well-to-do southerners lived much to his liking. He had now outlived two wives, still played tennis regularly, supported local charities, and on sunny weekends journeyed aboard his yacht from Biloxi to his slip at the Grand Hotel on Mobile Bay. With Gardiner Green and the late Alexander Field Chisholm, who had married his wife's cousin, he had been a major figure in directing the family's fortunes; and since Chisholm's death in 1973 he and Green had run the show pretty much by themselves.

Besides heading the Pascagoula Hardwood Company, Hynson had been the vice-president of Central Oil until its recent sale. Currently his most pressing interest was developing shopping centers on various Laurel properties, including the huge downtown site where the family's lumber mill had stood. Most of these enterprises, with the partial exception of Pascagoula Hardwood, were closely held family enterprises, autocratically run in the traditional way of small town family businesses (too traditionally and too autocratically, in the view of some younger members of the clan). Hynson frequently laments the stockholders' lack of interest in the various Laurel businesses, but he is sometimes blamed for not keeping them informed. An annual director's meeting and occasional telephone polls are the usual means of transmitting decisions. Perhaps it was this communications problem that had prompted Wayne Jackson, Graham Wisner's mentor, to report to Dave Morine in December, 1973, that shareholders and even the directors were not being kept abreast of the then imminent sale to Masonite. One member of the family observes, "Bob Hynson is an effective diplomat, an intermediary, but he's disorganized as a business-man. He doesn't take enough trouble with details or getting reports out on time. You'd have a hard time finding out from him the breakdowns about how much it costs to run a business." To which Hynson replies that the businesses have done very well over the years—all of them, that is, except the Pascagoula Hardwood Company, which had never shown a profit; but even it promised to be a bonanza if and when it was ever sold.

In any event, the problem of communications was once again raised now that Quisenberry's junkets and the progress of H.B. 914 were becoming widely known. This time, Hynson reacted swiftly. In March, 1975, having just returned from his meeting with Quisenberry at the River Hills Tennis Club in Jackson, he called a stockholders meeting at which Quisenberry and Morine would present their views of the state's and the Conservancy's intentions. On March 5, while H.B. 914 was beginning its suspenseful journey through the Mississippi Senate, some twenty-five or thirty stockholders were gathered at the Lauren Rogers Library and Museum of Art—a dignified Georgian edifice dedicated by one of the family's founders to his only grandson, Jane Hynson's cousin, who had died young. Here, surrounded by the eclectic dona-tions of family members—including a marvelous collection of hand-woven baskets, an assortment of paintings ranging from Corot, Homer, Inness, and Constable to the never-heard-of, sets of fine silver, and a suit of sixteenth-century armor—Quisenberry showed his film and Morine, fresh from his outburst before Senator Bodron's Finance Committee, expounded upon the tract's importance to the state and the conser-vancy's good intentions regarding a just remuneration to stockholders. The audience response was friendly. None of these people had received a dividend from the company in years, so they were inclined to view the proceeds of a sale as an unexpected windfall. But they were also impressed by Quisenberry's film; since few of them had ever visited the swamp, its beauty and ecological importance took them by surprise. At the end of the meeting, several shareholders told Quisenberry that they particularly hoped the tract would go to the state, thereby ensuring its preservation.

Morine and Quisenberry realized that they had been missing a bet. As Quisenberry would obseve, "In dealing with Hynson and Green we had figured that they were informing the rank and file of what was going on, but they were not. Now that these people had a better understanding of what we were trying to do, they were on our side. Most would have been happy to settle for hard cash. The company's directors would have to deal with that from now on."

Hynson, observing the audience's interest, was thinking the same thing. Pascagoula Hardwood Company was unique among the family assets in that it included so many nonfamily shareholders, and he had wondered how he could advise them of their best course of action when he had no idea of their financial circumstances. Now they were in effect advising him: they would not oppose the sale. "Our Laurel stockholders were top-heavy with garden club women, so naturally the film appealed to them," Hynson observes, adding drily, "I never saw such a beautiful film of a swamp—not a mosquito or a snake in sight!" He himself still had grave reservations. The provisions of a sale would have to afford him the necessary tax breaks and he was still doubtful that the state's legislators, "that bunch of dolts," would ever let H.B. 914 get through the Senate. Nevertheless, he was now conscious that the growing momentum in support of the swamp's preservation would be difficult to resist. Also, although he frankly admits that "my pocketbook comes ahead of my ecological conscience," that conscience had been stirred. Morine could not guess his thoughts—Hynson was "playing 'possum" —but for the first time the president of Pascagoula Hardwood was beginning to think that, if the terms could be worked out, a deal with the state might not be altogether a bad thing. Still, he was pretty certain that it would never come to that.

The next important event in Morine's dealings with the Pascagoula Hardwood Company took place on April 2, 1975, in New York City. H.B. 914 had survived its legislative trials and was now awaiting the governor's signature. This fact was duly noted by the Chisholm family, whose business manager, Jean Gardiner Chisholm Lindsey, had been present at the stock-holders' meeting in Laurel a month earlier. Jean Lindsey and Morine had agreed it was time that he addressed the other members of her family.

When Morine speaks of the Pascagoula transaction, he refers repeatedly to the "Four Families" with whom he had to deal—the Wisners, Hynsons, Greens, and Chisholms. In fact, the mostly female children of the Gardiner brothers and their only sister (who had remained in the Midwest) founded more families than these—Reeders, Coxes, Hulsts, Rogerses among them; but in terms of his own dealings with the clan, Morine's designation is accurate enough. Gardiner Green controlled about 24 percent of the Pascagoula Hardwood stock; Bob Hynson owned or controlled 18 percent; the Chisholms owned about 12 percent; and the Wisners, 8 percent. The latter two families were particularly close. Until his death in 1972, Alexander Field Chisholm had looked after the Wisner family interests in Laurel as well as his own. The ties between the families were additionally strengthened when his oldest daughter, Jean Lindsey, moved with her two young sons to Washington after she and her husband were divorced. For these and other reasons, the Chisholms and Wisners tended to represent one faction in the extended family's business ventures, while the Greens and Hynsons represented another—although Hynson, true to his role as intermediary, was often, as he says, "in the middle."

There had been considerable disagreement between Chisholm and Green, the president of Central Oil Compnay, about how that company should be managed. Exasperated by Green's conservatism, Chisholm —who had earlier purchased the mineral rights on vast tracts of land in southern Mississippi—set up his own oil business, the Brandon Company. The conservative chief executive of Laurel's First National Bank became a wildcatter in what was to prove a highly successful venture.

Chisholm had died before Morine appeared on the scene, but the man's enterprising spirit had been reincarnated in his remarkable daughter, Jean Lindsey. Until 1972, she had been, like Graham's mother, a Washington hostess and an active participant in the "Camelot" atmosphere of the Kennedy years. Now she determined to manage her father's affairs for herself and her two sisters, although her only training for the job derived from her experience on the boards of various Washington charities. She began taking night courses in business, asked a lot of questions of her associates, and reestablished Laurel as her home base. Her main interest was the Brandon Company, but she also took an active role in other family enterprises—too active, perhaps, to suit the taste of her "uncles," Green and Hynson, who sometimes felt that she lacked confidence in them and their decisions. "These were old southern family businesses," she explains, "You know; you start out buying the land for its timber, and that leads to mineral rights and oil, and then you're into real estate development. And all of it run by one or two family members who are used to making decisions on their own without consulting other people. Whereas I had been out in the big bad world. I came back to Laurel with a different preparation. I felt that nothing substitutes for people getting around a table and talking about things."

When Dave Morine asked if he could discuss the implications of H.B. 914 with her, Ms. Lindsey agreed that the time had come to get around a table. The meeting took place in the New York City apartment of her sister and brother-in-law, Cynthia and Nathan Saint-Amand, overlooking Central Park. Also on hand was the third of the Chisholm daughters, Margaret Ann Boxley, as well as the family's New York attorney, and representatives of the United States Trust Company which handled the Chisholm estate—"a lot of ritzy people," as Morine cheerfully phrases it. He had brought along a print of Quisenberry's film. At the press of a button, a screen materialized from the ceiling between two rooms. A moment later the elegant interior was displaced by images of shimmering swamp water, lofty cypress trees, bounding deer. Luckily for him, Morine allowed the film to speak for itself. Later,

Jean Lindsey would say, "Truly, one thing I don't like is to have people talk to me as though I don't know anything about the swamp. When we were young we used to take day trips down there quite often. I was always historically oriented; I knew there were Indian mounds and all that sort of thing. We were always interested in that part of the country from an idealistic as well as business point of view."

Morine had met Ms. Lindsey once or twice before, but this was the first real opportunity to take her measure—as she was certainly taking his. He was impressed. She was an attractive woman in a suede business suit, carefully groomed, with dark auburn hair and beautiful hands that were rarely still. When she spoke it was with the assumption that she would be listened to. Morine had been several times warned that she could be cold and quick to put others down. For his part, he felt at ease with her; he liked her no-nonsense attitude and tough questions. "When the film was over," he recalls, "Jean turns to me and says, 'Well, David, we all agree that it's a very pretty piece of property, and we're all sympathetic with what you're trying to do. Now let's get down to business.' By God, she grilled me; about the Conservancy, about bargain sales, about how the federal tax exemptions worked for donations. Nothing was going to get by her if she could help it."

Morine outlined the advantages of a bargain sale. Complex in its details, the general concept was clear enough. If an individual or corporation sells a property to a nonprofit organization for less than the land's appraised fair market value, they can claim the difference between the lower "bargain sale" price and the fair market value as a charitable donation. This donation can be subtracted from their taxable income, which often results in an after-tax return that compares favorably with a sale on the open market.

After two hours of exploring such possibilities, Ms. Lindsey decided that she had heard everything she needed to know. She told Morine that her family would in fact be interested in considering a bargain sale of their interest in Pascagoula Hardwood. Specifically, she tentatively agreed to consider the $15 million pro-rate share figure regardless of the fair market value of the tract. Morine left the apartment in a jubilant mood. This was the first real break in the detachment of any of the Four Families. He assumed that the Chisholms' decision was motivated by the family's need for ready cash with which to settle their father's estate, but Jean Lindsey discounts this. "I'm always interested in any business proposal," she says. "We liked the idea; we thought it was a good deal. What we told David was that it seemed fair from a business point of view and it would keep the land together in perpetuity. I'm not portraying us as saintly types, but our decision was weighted by our feeling for that part of the country. It was the preservation aspect that appealed to us."

Jean Lindsey also felt that she had a more acute sense of historical necessity than her Laurel relatives. She was a political lobbyist herself on occasion, and had followed the campaign to launch H.B. 914 more with admiration than alarm. "Early on, I was aware that a momentum was building. . . . A lot of the family didn't realize how these things were done. They were surprised that the legislative vote was so unanimous—but I felt that the whole lobbying effort, bringing the politicians down to see the swamp, and so forth, was intelligently done. Of course, I *was* surprised that the state people went down there and made that movie without asking. In any case, I felt that once the bill was passed, we needed to know what we were going to do. I think I had a sense that the time was ripe."

Morine's sense of euphoria was tempered by the awareness that, in itself, the Chisholm family's twelve percent of the stock meant very little. By this time he knew that the Nature Conservancy would have to act not only as middleman but also as actual purchaser in any transaction with the Pascagoula Hardwood Company. Short of an outright sale of the land—to which Hynson and Green seemed unalterably opposed— there was no way that Mississippi could take possession of the property directly, since the state was prohibited by law from acquiring the corporation or its stock. Morine was now in the same bind that Graham Wisner had been caught in when he dreamed of translating his 1 percent of the stock into 1 percent of the land: how to convert shares into land when there were 110 stockholders to be considered? The Conservancy would not want to buy the Chisholms' 12 percent interest in the swamp as an isolated unit; but even if it did, how could it be done? Which percent of the tract was the Chisholms'? It was like trying to divide a house between several heirs without first selling it.

A month and a half later, on May 19, it was the Wisners' turn to meet with Morine. As with the Chisholms, the family was gathered in full force for the occasion, again at a fashionable address, the yellow brick Georgetown mansion of Graham's mother, now the wife of well-known socialite and *Washington Post* columnist Clayton Fritchie. The library was set up for the occasion—folding chairs and the inevitable projection screen crowding the Greek statuary and antique furniture, but without noticeably diminishing the elegance of the book-lined room. Here were gathered Graham, his older brothers, Frank and Ellis, his sister, Wendy (who shared Graham's counterculture outlook), their imposing mother, several lawyers, and, again, representatives of the U.S. Trust Company, which handled the Wisners', as well as the Chisholms', affairs. Morine had brought his boss, Pat Noonan, with him to "give weight" to his presentation.

This was the first time that this branch of the "Four Families" had been formally approached about the possible sale of their Pascagoula holdings. During the presentation of the film and the questioning that followed, Morine noticed that in these surroundings Graham Wisner was much quieter and more conservatively dressed than was his usual wont. The young man would afterwards say, "I was deliberately reserved that day; I made a conscious decision not to try to run the meeting." Morine's interpretation was somewhat different. He was disappointed that Graham was not supporting the project, here in the bosom of his family, with the same enthusiasm he had shown at the meeting with Governor Waller and his aides in Jackson. "Now that he was on his home turf," says Morine, "it was obvious that he wasn't such a honcho anymore. When you came to Mother's house, by God, you played by Mother's rules: you got dressed up in a coat and tie, and sat in the corner with your sister like a good little boy."

There was little opportunity, however, to savor these undercurrents of feeling. After Noonan and Morine had described the ecological importance of the Pascagoula, and dwelt at some length on the attractions of bargain sales and tax write-offs, the hard questions began. Frank Wisner, Jr. and the U.S. Trust people contributed their share, but it was obvious that here, as at the Saint-Amand apartment, a single personality dominated the discussion. This was J. Ellis Knowles Wisner, the middle brother and chief administrator of the family's fortunes. Tall, expensively groomed, with a narrow, thoughtful face, he was one of the least knowable figures with whom Morine would have to deal.

Wisner was a bona fide intellectual, with a highly cultivated interest in the arts, particularly music. After graduating from Yale, he took a Bachelor of Letters at Oxford (his thesis dealt with the influence of Heraclitus on Hegel and Nietzsche). He headed the Washington Opera Guild, had a trained voice himself, and occasionally sang for cancer patients at the National Institute of Health. These cultural and altruistic interests coexisted in his life with more pragmatic activities. While Graham demonstrated against the Vietnam War, Ellis was in Vietnam with the U.S. Agency for International Development. While his older brother Frank pursued a career in the State Department, Ellis became the successive trustee, after the death of his uncle Field Chisholm, for the family's financial affairs. He had the Wisner grace and could charm anyone when he wished to; but he was circumspect when dealing with people he did not know. Generalizations or rash moves were not in his line; his conversation was qualified by phrases such as, "That is too simple," or "What's to be said?" or "I don't know what I thought."

The sale of the Pascagoula was a prospect about which Ellis Wisner did not know what to think. Until the advent of H.B. 914, he had not taken the overtures of the state and the Nature Conservancy very seriously, though he felt, like Jean Lindsey, that he was not as informed as he wished to be about what was going on in Laurel. Now that pressure for the sale was building, his mind, conditioned to see all sides of an issue, saw perhaps more than he wished. He was attracted by the altruistic appeal to do something for Mississippi, which gave weight to Morine and Noonan's presentation, although, in a typically circuitous sentence, he would later explain that he was, "after all, not born in Mississippi, and could not be said to have roots there; at any rate not in the hackneyed sense that the word has taken on."

On the other hand, he felt some pang of loss now that the Wisners' economic ties with the state were being cut. Pascagoula Hardwood was one of the few Mississippi enterprises in which his family still had an interest. If it too were sold, "we would be divesting ourselves of yet another family business—minor, but not insignificant in terms of what the Gardiners had built when they came down to Laurel." With a faint melancholy, he observes that "we were approaching the end of the level of personal control, that is, of closely held corporate business—which is what so often happens in the fourth generation. I don't want to make too big a deal of this, but we did have a tie with Laurel and this was obviously diminishing. For us, the sale of the Pascagoula would mark the end of an era."

Sentiment aside, however, Wisner realized that the sale offered a chance to get out of an investment that paid no dividends, that he privately believed to be poorly managed, and over which he could exercise little control. Nor was he enamoured of the idea, so vigorously promoted in Laurel two years earlier, of selling the company to another corporation for an exchange of stock. Morine and Noonan did not fail to remind him and his family that Masonite shares were now worth much less than they had been, and that the Wisners would have taken a heavy loss if that sale had gone through. From the tax point of view, the deal Morine was proposing would be most advantageous to Ellis's mother, because of her high income bracket, and least advantageous to his younger brother, Graham, and sister, Elizabeth, because their incomes were considerably less. But Graham and Elizabeth were the two members of the family who wholeheartedly supported Morine's effort to preserve the swamp.

Ellis Wisner's own attitude was equivocal: "I *think* I am not a person who believes that nature, *in this sense*, is the paramount interest. No interest is paramount." In the same all-sided way, he felt that no interest was wholly pure. The House amendment which would have allowed the State Forestry Commission to manage the swamp had left him skeptical of the state's motives. Now, when he thinks of those reservations, he existentially concludes, "I don't believe anything in life is unalloyed. I think you always have to give up some things to gain others. What we would give up if we went along with the sale—which was considerable— would have to be outweighed by the returns both in terms of money and the fact that we were doing something good."

At the end of this meeting, Morine and Noonan came away with nothing promised. Yet both men sensed that the Wisner family would not oppose the sale as long as they did not lose by it. Ellis Wisner concedes that "it must have been about then that we realized we might go along with the deal. That meeting meant that we would commit time to it."

Whatever the headway being made in Washington and New York, in Laurel, nothing, at least on the surface, had changed. During 1976, Morine was averaging a trip to Mississippi every month. He always stopped in Jackson where he conferred with Avery Wood and Quisenberry and sometimes met with the Heritage Committee. But he was usually enroute to Laurel, where he and Hynson and Gardiner Green would "go round and around" in a series of negotiations that always seemed to end up where they had begun, "which was nowhere." Morine would observe frequently that he liked these people, and sometimes regretted that his meetings with them were "strictly business." As individuals, the members of the clan certainly interested him, but their collective identity intrigued him too. He had his fair share of the traditional American schizophrenia concerning inherited wealth. He rejoiced in his own capacities as a self-made man and regarded anyone who was not ambitious as being somehow underprivileged, whether they were rich or poor. Yet he was paradoxically drawn, in a romantic, F. Scott Fitzgerald sort of way, to the "old money" of certain eastern and southern families—or, more exactly, to the sense of self-assurance that it instilled in those who had it. Obsessed as he was by the desire to pry the Pascagoula loose from the Four Families' hold, he envied them their attitude toward a prospective sale—their underlying view that, whatever they might or might not decide, they didn't *have* to do anything.

For their part, the representatives of the Four Families regarded Morine retrospectively in a unanimously friendly light. They describe him as "energetic," "personable," "dedicated;" and they acknowledge that his ability to make himself liked had some influence on their decisions. They tend to remember him in hospitable terms, as though he had been their frequent houseguest and dinner companion as well as a gifted salesman promoting an idea. In fact, however, the social amenities, to the extent that they existed, belonged only to the last stage of two years of negotiations. During most of that time, when Morine was not in the offices or conference room of the Eastman-Gardiner Building, or sitting on the bench outside, he was either driving to or from Jackson, or else holed up in Laurel's Town House Motor Hotel (one of the families' properties) waiting for the next conference to begin. Unlike Quisenberry, he was a professional traveler, but even he was not altogether immune to pangs of homesickness when yet another appointment in Laurel separated him from his pretty wife, Ruth, and their comfortable home in Great Falls, Virginia, on special occasions, a Thanksgiving Day or a wedding anniversary. Also during 1975, his commitment to the Pascagoula deal was shadowed by an impending personal tragedy. His mother, a strong-willed woman to whom he owed much of his sense of social consciousness, was dying of cancer. "She understood why I couldn't see her as often as I wanted to. There was never any question between us about what I had to do. Basically, I felt that I was opposing something negative, death, with something positive, something that would last. Still," he adds, "I felt bad, being far away from her so much of the time."

It must be remembered that Morine was now working under enormous pressure. Avery Wood, Quisenberry, legislators like Deaton and Strider, and the people of Mississippi had all done their part. The funding that was asked for had been produced, and there was a widespread expectation that the swamp would soon pass into public ownership. At Morine's suggestion, the Heritage Committee was even now in the process of hiring appraisers to determine the real value of the tract. Wood, with his incorrigible enthusiasm and his almost mystical faith in Morine, was certain that the deal would go through. A few others, like Quisenberry, were less sanguine, but even they could not understand fully the difficulty of Morine's position. During 1975, not only the state of Mississippi but the Nature Conservancy as well, would commit its energies and large sums of money to his project. "I did almost too good a job of getting my own troops in line," he reflects. He had brought in Graham Wisner and Quisenberry's film to convince the staff of the importance of the Pascagoula; and he later delivered an impassioned speech to the Conservancy's Board of Governors at one of their quarterly meetings. Indeed, he had become so carried away on the latter occasion that he all but promised them he would "deliver the goods." In response to this enthusiasm, the Conservancy had already invested tens of thousands of dollars in the Mississippi Heritage Program and would soon provide a hundred thousand more—for the inventory program, Morine's time and expenses, attorney fees and the like—without any guarantee that there would be a return on the investment. The commitment was not a reckless one; after all, miracles had already been achieved in the state legislature; and among the Four Families one was receptive to a sale and another would probably go along. But the risk was nevertheless very great. The Laurel faction, represented by Hynson and Gardiner Green, remained the immovable object, and it was becoming increasingly clear that Green, in particular, with his control of almost a fourth of Pascagoula Hardwood stock, was the blocking interest.

Gardiner Green enjoys fishing and partying at his weekend retreat— a relatively modest establishment for so wealthy a man—at Point Clear on Mobile Bay. And in his younger days he used to play bridge for high stakes. But all who know him agree that his one true passion is making money. If Dave Morine likes to make deals better than anything else in the world, it is possible that Gardiner Green likes to make deals even more than that. In his case, that pleasure is not infringed upon by extraneous considerations like "making everybody feel good" or becoming sentimental about family holdings. One plays to win. On the other hand there is probably nothing that he hates more than taxes, and any deal that involves him must include safeguards against the depredations of the Internal Revenue Service.

From all reports, he can be pleasant company in a social setting, where he likes to talk about the general state of the economy—especially what the government is doing wrong—very much; but he plays a close hand where his own business interests are concerned, rarely discussing them even with Bob Hynson; nor does he like his decisions to be questioned. Hynson has always respected this secretiveness, with the result that the two men still act in harmony with each other. But the Chisholms and Wisners have been less obliging. Because of fundamental differences in their business philosophies, the late Field Chisholm and Gardiner Green were often at odds. Since Chisholm's death, both his daughter and Ellis Wisner have frequently questioned the way Green and Hynson have managed the Laurel interests of their respective families. "Those myriad questions gave us the feeling that they were accusatory," Hynson says. "Questions always imply that something is wrong."

The basic issue was whether Hynson, and particularly Green, were perhaps too unaggressive and too autocratic in managing the family enterprises. In Field Chisholm's day, the disagreement over policy, and Green's feeling that he was no longer able to control the decision-making process, had led to the sale of Central Oil. Now, the Pascagoula Hardwood Company had become the focus of the continuing dispute. With the exception of one year, it had never returned a dividend; timber operations had almost ceased; efforts to sell it for an exchange of stock had failed; and it had become, in effect, an inactive corporation.

Some younger members of the clan felt frustrated by the unhurried, wait-and-see attitude of the Laurel directors, and they held Green chiefly accountable. "You get the feeling that Gardiner wants to turn the clock back," says one of them. "He's created an environment in which people do what he wants. He feels people are antagonistic if they ask questions. There are people who brag that they've got something for nothing, but when you look more closely you see that they've lost out somewhere else. Basically, he's not really attuned to living in the modern economic climate."

These tensions did not prevent the Four Families from acting in tandem when their mutual interests were involved. Morine, in his dealings with them, perceived no dissension or conflicts of interest at all. His estimate of Green is frankly admiring: "Gardiner has a tremendous understanding of the value of finite resources. He believes in doing nothing, an interesting philosophy, which in his case is correct. He doesn't need cash so he just lets the world appreciate around him. Of course, for stockholders who are not in that position, it is an exasperating attitude. It's also exasperating if you want to do business with him."

Hynson also weighs in on Green's side. "Let's face it," he says, "Gardiner is the cagiest bargainer you'd ever have to deal with. Unlike me he has a bargaining instinct in his nature. . . . But he's also a fantastic analyzer. He'll sit at his desk at the office and study figures for hours. He's got to be shown how his interests are enhanced by a deal."

Morine had more than his share of coping with Green's bargaining skills. He admits he was led astray by the assumption that Green was, from the first, simply horsetrading, holding out for a better price for the Pascagoula tract. "In fact, Gardiner was being totally honest and consistent in saying he didn't want to sell for cash. I assumed that anyone will compromise. I'd done a thousand deals aiming for the compromise. But I'd never met the likes of Gardiner Green." Actually, Green did contribute somewhat to this misapprehension. Once, when Jean Lindsey suggested at a board meeting that the directors really ought to let Morine know where they stood, "Gardiner looked at me as though I was from Mars."

Green did repeatedly advise Morine that the latter should press for a division of the property in which those who wanted to sell could, and those who didn't, needn't. But at the same time, he made clear that he would sell for cash if the price were high enough. Early one morning in

April, 1975, when he, Hynson, and Morine were once again conferring at the Laurel office building, he took out a pencil and calculated, for Morine's benefit, that in order to get the same after-tax benefit from a cash sale to the Conservancy which he would have gotten from the $15 million stock exchange with Masonite, he would have to ask $22 million for the property. The seeming extravagance of this figure helped to convince Morine that Green was indeed horsetrading, and that a compromise price could be reached.

With this end in mind, Morine argued that there could be no decision about price until the real value of the land was determined. He told Green and Hynson that the Mississippi Heritage Committee was already arranging for three independent appraisers to evaluate the value of the tract. Morine claimed that if the state provided the only appraisals, the figure they came up with would become public knowledge, and the company directors would be "locked in" to that figure whether they wanted to be or not. Gardiner Green's first inclination was to resist this line of argument. The momentum in favor of a sale, which Jean Lindsey and Ellis Wisner had decided not to oppose, and which had impressed even Hynson, was to Green tantamount to an invasion of privacy. He had been scandalized by the sheer publicity of the enterprise, the involvement of the public and the media, the unexpected passage of H.B. 914, the sheer audacity and openness of Morine's approach. Furthermore, he had been furious at the governor's intercession in the negotiations with International Paper, and felt under no obligation to help the state or the Conservancy to achieve their aims.

However, at this point Hynson introduced a troubling subject—the same one that he had broached to Quisenberry a month earlier, namely, the threat of condemnation. Both he and Green were as worried as Morine that the state's appraisal figures might be low, but for a different reason: they feared that in the event the state condemned the land, those figures might be used to determine its fair market value. They asked Morine whether the prospect of condemnation was likely. He replied, as Quisenberry had, that Mississippi was not considering such a move, at least not yet. Privately, he was as skeptical as Quisenberry that the legislature would ever consider so extreme an action, though, knowing Avery Wood, he did not discount it altogether. For the benefit of his listeners, he urged that even the possibility of condemnation was a sufficient reason for an independent appraisal which the company could have ready "when the state appraisers come parading into the office."

Hynson and Green finally admitted the logic of this suggestion, even accepting Morine's recommendation as to whom the appraiser should be, a Michigan specialist in woodland real estate, Bud Cannon, who had previously done work for the Conservancy.

The Pascagoula transaction was becoming curiouser and curiouser. Not only had money been raised to buy the property before the proposed sellers were committed or even interested, but now the would-be buyer, far from seeking a bargain, was as eager as the would-be sellers to arrive at a maximum fair market value for the land. There was no question that this was Morine's intent: "I was scared to death that the state appraisers might lack the perspective to understand the land's real value. If they came in with a low figure, maybe 14 or 15 million, Hynson and Green would say 'screw you,' and the deal would be dead. I figured that an unbiased appraisal would show a value of at least $18 million. If they would go for that, splitting the difference between the 15 million I've got and the 22 million Green was asking for—in other words, if we agreed on 18 million—I was certain I could talk them out of the $3 million difference as a tax benefit. They couldn't lose. If they sold the land at a bargain sale price, 15 million, and it was appraised at 18 million, the 3 million would be a charitable donation to the Conservancy, a nonprofit organization; and, given these people's high income brackets, they would have a terrific tax write-off. Since there would be no middle man's commission, and we could pay hard cash—hell, there was no way we couldn't make this deal fly." Or so he thought.

Morine took no chances. With Hynson's and Green's approval, he had Quisenberry arrange a meeting in Jackson attended by Bud Cannon, the three Mississippi appraisers hired by the state—Jack Mann, Ed Turner, and T. J. Carraway—and the man who would undertake a timber cruise (an evaluation of timber value only). William May. Cannon had already produced his general estimate of value, which came to $17.5 million for the tract. This disappointed Morine since it was not quite enough to cover the tax write-off benefits he planned to offer the company. More to the point, he was concerned that this estimate would influence the subsequent estimates by the state's appraisers. He feared that they might come in at $17.5 or even less. At the Jackson meeting, therefore, Morine deliberately stressed the fact that the tract was unique, and that its recreational and ecological importance should be figured into the cost. The appraisers agreed to keep these considerations in mind.

Meanwhile, in his dealing with Hynson and Green, Morine was becoming "a burnt-out case." During the summer of 1975 he called on the Conservancy's head, Pat Noonan, "to come in as a second team." The two of them visited Laurel together in mid-July and Noonan tried the hard sell: "We'd sat on the bench; now we were in Hynson's office," Morine remembers. "Pat tells Green and Hynson we are really going to make them a deal; this is going to put Mississippi on the map. As astute businessmen they must realize that their families owed a lot to Mississippi, and it's time to give something back; that we operate in a wonderful free country with a free enterprise system; we aren't urging condemnation; we aren't ramming anything down their throats, etcetera. It was a real pep talk. To which they reply, 'The property is worth 22 million, period.' Hynson did concede that America was a great place, but Gardiner Green wasn't even going to admit that. He thinks the country has gone to hell. The meeting lasted an hour, a one-way conversation to nowhere. When we got back in our rented car, I'm feeling dead; but Pat just laughed and said, 'Those guys are *tough!* ' "

Noonan had another crack at Green in September. During the Conservancy board meeting, at which Morine had delivered his impassioned and successful request for continuing support of the Pascagoula project, one of the board members, Mrs. W. Lyon Brown, had volunteered the fact that she was a good friend of Gardiner Green's wife, Eleanor, through their mutual association with the influential Garden

Clubs of America, of which Mrs. Green was vice-president. At her request, the Greens extended an invitation to Noonan for an overnight stay at their home on Laurel's Fifth Avenue. The visit was cordial but unproductive. However, soon after, Green wrote Noonan requesting more information on bargain sales and how they could be used for tax write-offs. "I had explained bargain sales to him until I was blue in the face," says Morine, "but I think maybe Gardiner enjoyed dealing with the big chief. Actually he wasn't interested in bargain sales or any other kind of sale. But we didn't know that. I still thought maybe he was going for a compromise. Anyway, this tiny ray of interest on his part encouraged us to go on."

During these months of negotiations, Morine gradually sensed that Bob Hynson, president of Pascagoula Hardwood, would probably come to terms with the Conservancy about a bargain sale if he was left to his own devices. But it was also clear that neither he nor any of the other stockholders would act against Gardiner Green's interests. Morine was convinced that if the stalemate was to be broken, he had to do something "out of the ordinary." He no longer remembers the moment when a possible solution to the impasse began to dawn on him. He had been knocking on a locked door for so long that it took him some time to realize that there might be another way of getting inside the house. This other way seems obvious enough now, but at the time it was an unprecedented approach for a nonprofit environmental group to take. He would give up the idea of buying the swamp. He would somehow buy the Pascagoula Hardwood Company instead. "I threw this out as an idea to Pat Noonan. None of us had ever done anything like this although it's a standard businessman's approach. So Pat's response was, 'Why not? Explore it.'"

Noonan's advice might sound casual, but exploring the idea meant the commitment of large quantities of Conservancy time and money. Morine journeyed to Chicago to consult with an expert in corporate law, Tom Healy, with whom the Conservancy had done business before. The two men discussed the various ways in which a corporation could be acquired and dissolved. Any such undertaking would involve a number of risks. Most of the 110 stockholders would have to be persuaded to sell, and there was no guarantee that they would— particularly if Gardiner Green took the lead in holding onto his share, which he seemed likely to do. Even if most of them were so persuaded, including Hynson, whose role as president of the company and con- troller of 18 percent of the shares was now crucial, how could the company's major asset, the swamp itself, be divided so that everyone, including those who would not sell their interests to the Conservancy, got a fair share when and if the company was bought and broken down? Furthermore, in buying the company instead of the land, the Conservancy would be buying "a pig in a poke," as Morine put it, since such a procedure would involve the acquisition of all assets (machinery, structures, etc.) and liabilities pertaining to Pascagoula Hardwood Company. Finally, the Conservancy would have to borrow the millions necessary to undertake the purchase of all available shares, then take possession of the company, divide the land with those who wouldn't sell, dissolve the company, and sell the tract to the state of Mississippi while all the time the interest on the original loan was adding up like the numbers in a ticking taxi meter. "If anything went wrong," says Morine, "we'd be up the creek."

It should be noted that at this point Morine was still thinking in terms of a sale in which not only Hynson but Green could be persuaded to take part. His chief motive in proposing to buy the company itself was to provide shareholders with yet another tax break. If the Conservancy bought only the land, the company would have been taxed on the capital gains; then, when the profits of the sale were distributed to stockholders, each individual would have to declare his share in in- come. In short, profits from the sale would be taxed twice. On the other hand, if a tender offer were accepted for the company itself, taxes would be levied only once, at the capital gains rate, on each stockholder according to the purchase price of his shares.

Even as Morine was investigating the possibilities of this approach during the last weeks of 1975, he was faced with yet another crisis. The state appraisers came in with their estimate: $22 million for the 42,000-acre tract—the very price that Gardiner Green had been demanding for some months past. This unexpectedly high figure was not, as it happened, evidence that the appraisers had been carried away by the idea of evaluating the land as an ecological treasure. Rather, the timber cruise had turned up an additional 90 million board feet of timber. (When Cannon had prepared his earlier estimate of value for the company, Green and Hynson had told him to assume that the tract contained 150 million board feet. The state's professional timber cruise indicated that a more exact figure would be 240 million board feet. Cannon had been accurate in his appraisal of the land value, but the increase in the estimate of timber, plus the effects of inflation, jumped the price by some $5 million.)

This new estimate was a devastating blow to Morine. He had wanted an increase in the appraisal, but the discrepancy between fair market value and the $15 million which the state had raised was now so great that not all the tax breaks in the world could bridge the gap. Morine, convinced at last that he was beaten, nevertheless made one last despairing bid. With the help of the Chicago attorney, Healy, he submitted a formal bid to Pascagoula Hardwood to buy the company for the now pitifully inadequate sum of $15 million.

In January, 1976, a little more than a year after he had received that first letter from Bob Hynson saying no to his original request for an option to buy the swamp, Morine received another letter saying no to his latest proposal. The only surprising thing about this letter was that a sentence had been included in it almost as an afterthought. Instead of closing the door once and for all, Hynson suggested that Morine should pursue the possibility of a deal further with his attorney in Jackson, a man named James P. Knight. Again and again Morine read that sentence, wondering what it could mean.

CHAPTER XI

Success

IRONICALLY, the new appraisal, which Morine regarded as a death blow to his efforts, was perceived by Hynson and Green in a quite different light. They were delighted to learn that Pascagoula Hardwood was worth $22 million. At that kind of price they were ready to deal. It remained for James Knight, the company's tax lawyer, to rearrange the pieces in the puzzle to form a new picture.

When Knight was apprised of the problems concerning the Pascagoula negotiations, he set to work to resolve them. He knew that Gardiner Green was still unwilling to sell his share of the company, or rather, the land which that share represented. He knew that, in any case, the Nature Conservancy and the state did not have enough money to buy the whole of the property. He knew that Morine could no longer hold to his fixation that, in some way, all 42,500 acres could be acquired. On the other hand, he also realized that the ecologically important bottomlands comprised only about three-quarters of the tract. And he soon learned that even if Green would not sell at the higher rate of value, the Chisholms, Wisners, and Hynson, would.

He was much intrigued by Morine's hypothesis that the Conservancy could make a tender offer to buy the company instead of the land, an idea which thus far had come to nothing. Suppose, Knight asked himself, that all of the shareholders except Green's faction could be persuaded to sell to the Conservancy? That would represent approximately 75 percent of the stock, at a theoretical price of more than $16.5 million. However, given the Conservancy's nonprofit status and the various tax breaks available to stockholders who sold at bargain prices, the actual price would be closer to $13 million. Once it acquired a majority interest, the Conservancy, with Green's consent, could dissolve the company, divide the land, and sell its share to the state. At that rate, Morine and eventually the state would get three-quarters of the tract at less than four-fifths of the originally proposed cost. As Knight would make clear to Morine, three-quarters of a loaf was much better than nothing at all. And the price, after all, was one that the buyer could afford and the seller would accept.

Between the conceptual stage of this eminently sane idea and its practical realization there intervened an armada of federal laws governing the dissolution of various types of companies under various circumstances, not to mention the human factor represented by a large number of minority shareholders who might or might not be willing to go along with the scheme. It was not the sort of venture that could be lightly undertaken. But Knight decided that it was worth a try.

On February 3, 1976, Knight, Dave Morine, the Conservancy's Chicago attorney, Thomas Healy, and some of the latter's colleagues, gathered in Healy's glassy office on the thirty-fifth floor of Chicago's La Salle Bank Building. Morine has a vivid recollection of this meeting: "I talked with Tom Healy and a couple of his associates before Jim Knight arrived. Tom tells me, 'Look, I've dealt with these country boys before. In all likelihood this guy won't know anything about how to structure the deal, so we'll have to walk him through.' Only that wasn't the way it happened. As it turned out, Knight was not only a lawyer, but also a CPA who had worked for the IRS for almost twenty years. Leave it to Gardiner Green the tax hater, to have found him! If you want to find your way around the chicken house, hire the top chicken! Anyway, Knight told us what we had to do. He and the others sat there for a couple of hours, Knight citing section such-and-such and case so-and-so, and all of them talking their lawyer mumbo-jumbo, with Knight right in there mumbo-jumboing with the best of them. When he was through with his presentation, I had nothing to say, and Healy and his associates simply nodded in complete agreement."

Knight had prepared himself for the meeting with care. He had reviewed the laws relating to the liquidation of corporations, he understood the tax status of the Nature Conservancy, and he could say that the Hynson, Chisholm, and Wisner interests would probably accept a tender offer of a bargain sale rate of $1,750 per share. Knight could also assure his listeners that if the Conservancy and Gardiner Green became co-owners of the company, the latter would not object to its dissolution providing an equitable division of the land was arranged—and provided also, of course, that the Internal Revenue Service would not object. This last was a tricky question; if Green could not extricate his share of the tract without paying taxes, he would certainly bolt. The tax code covering this issue was extremely technical, and permitted liquidations "only within a rather narrow range," as Knight phrases it. Knight was pretty certain that he had covered all contingencies on this subject, but even so, he stipulated that an IRS ruling on the tax consequences of liquidating the company would have to be acquired before the deal went through. This precaution was agreed to by all parties, and then put aside, where it remained for some months, ticking like a time bomb waiting to explode.

For their part, Morine and Healy stipulated that fully 75 percent of the company's shares must come into the Conservancy's hands in order for the deal to be binding. Their reasoning was that the success of the sale must be made contingent upon the cooperation of virtually all minority stockholders; if not, some of them might be tempted to follow Gardiner Green's example, trying to translate their shares into land too. If that happened, of course, it would complicate still more the difficult business of dividing up the property and at the same time it would further diminish the Nature Conservancy's share.

With these conditions accepted by both sides, Healy and Knight agreed to work together in drawing up a letter of intent, obligating Pascagoula Hardwood not to negotiate with anyone else while the tender offer was prepared.

So the meeting ended, with the Conservancy and Pascagoula Hardwood closer to a workable deal than they had ever been before. There were still obstacles enough: reaching an agreement with Green about how the land should be divided; convincing the small stockholders that they should sell; and getting Wood, Quisenberry, Deaton, and the other state people to run the legislative gauntlet again in order to tailor a new appropriations bill, involving less money but also a lot less land, to the terms of the proposed transaction. Still, an agreement of sorts had at long last been reached. Morine came away a little dazed. The idea of buying the company and liquidating it in lieu of a land purchase had originally been his; but he had not expected it to come about in this way. True, he had won, albeit not as much as he had hoped to win; but it was Gardiner Green who had the last laugh. Morine ruefully remembered the day in Laurel, nearly two years earlier, when Green had pointed to a map of the Pascagoula tract and told him he should think of some way to divide the land, instead of trying to buy all of it. At the time Morine had dismissed the idea, yet here he was, after so long a time, adopting it as his own. Well, he mused, it was just as Knight had suggested: three-quarters of a loaf was much better than none at all. The thought cheered him considerably.

A month later, on March 2, Morine and Quisenberry met with the state appraisers and the Pascagoula Hardwood forestry consultant, James M. Vardaman, who was now representing Gardiner Green's interests. The purpose of the meeting was to see who got what part of the loaf. Both Morine and Quisenberry remembered this session as a singularly unpleasant one. Whether because Vardaman had been instructed by Green to take a very hard line, or because he did so on his own initiative, he proved to be intractable as a negotiator. Actually, no real negotiations took place. Vardaman knew that he held all the cards. Luckily, his inflexibility had no calamitous consequences since the divisioning, at Vardaman's dictation, followed pretty much the pine land-bottomland distinction that both sides counted on. True, the ensuing layout of the partitioned land, especially at the southern border, was not as neat as Morine would have wished, but he and the state could live with that. It was the tone of the meeting that left him and Quisenberry with a bad taste in their mouths. There was no room for discussion, no hope of compromise even on the smallest points. Still, it was soon over; and however one-sided the process, an acceptable divisioning of the land had been accomplished.

On the same day, Morine signed a letter of intent to Pascagoula Hardwood confirming the Conservancy's intention to buy the company. And again on the same day, Representative Deaton wrote the Conservancy, at Morine's suggestion, officially requesting that the organization buy the tract for the state of Mississippi.

Now that Morine had described the terms of the potential sale, Wood and the members of the Wildlife Heritage Committee were moving into high gear again. H.B. 914 would have to be amended to conform to the new price and acreage, and there was little time to lose. This new effort paralleled the original plan to enact H.B. 914—Quisenberry stepped up the number of his speaking engagements, Avery Wood resumed his lobbying efforts, and Deaton, Strider, and other Heritage Committee members undertook to guide the new bill on another journey through the legislature. But if the scenario was much the same, many of the actors were not. Waller had recently been succeeded by a new governor, Cliff Finch, an unknown quantity as far as environmental issues were concerned. The legislature was also a very different place. Mississippians, in keeping with the decade's general dissatisfaction with political incumbents, had voted some 40 percent of them out of office. A comparable changeover had occurred in the makeup of the Heritage Committee. The new members were Donald Cumbest and Judge Francis Bowling, chosen by Governor Finch, and Senator Sam Wright and Representative Donald Cross replacing Ray Montgomery and "Farmer" Jim Neal respectively.

Only Representatives Deaton and Gollott, Senators Strider and Rhodes, and Coach John Vaught were still in place. So was Avery Wood, but only just barely. As a political appointee of the Waller administration, his days were numbered. It had taken him a while to realize this, given his temperamental inability to think in terms of political expediency; indeed, he still believes that if he had promised to be "obedient" to the interests of the incoming administration, he might have been kept on. As it was, he was not displaced until October, 1976. "They needed six votes out of the eleven Game and Fish commissioners to kick me out," he says, "and it took them that long to get me." By March, however, he realized that they would "get him" eventually, and he was "fighting an organized retreat." He was trying to "lock" some of his staff into their jobs, notably Quisenberry and his deputy director, George Chandler, so they couldn't be ousted or demoted; and—as he frequently told Morine—he wanted deperately to see the Pascagoula deal concluded before he left office. In any case, Wood, Quisenberry, and the new and old members of the Heritage Committe made another all-out effort in behalf of the new appropriations bill, and, in spite of some effectively organized opposition on the part of hunting clubs in the Pascagoula area, they were successful once again. On May 2, 1976, the bill, authorizing $13.5 million in general obligation funds to purchase 32,000 acres of the Pascagoula Swamp, was passed by the legislature.

The conditions of the tender offer involved several fairly exacting cutoff dates. The stock of virtually all shareholders except the Green family had to be tendered by May 14. The IRS ruling had to be received—it was assumed that it would be favorable since Knight and Healy had researched the matter thoroughly—by mid-July, in order to allow for the sale of Pascagoula Hardwood to the Conservancy by August 10, 1976, the date specified in the tender offer as the final date for concluding the transaction.

Each individual stockholder was sent a tender offer for his share of stock. In this procedure, Bob Hynson's help proved invaluable. Having made up his mind that the offer was a fair one and that preservation of the swamp was important, he lent it all the support he could. In the weeks following the issuance of the offer, he was besieged by phone calls from shareholders wanting to know what they ought to do. Again and again he described the reasons for the offer, explained the potential tax breaks, and, as head of the company, advised that they go along with the proposal. Gardiner Green was also helpful. Though still skeptical that the sale would be accomplished, he had yielded so far to Morine's

persuasion and the advice of Knight that he agreed to sell—if necessary
—as many as 135 of his own shares to provide an edge for the
Conservancy in the event that one or two recalcitrant stockholders with
a handful of shares refused to turn them loose.

Even with this edge, the process of purchasing shares from more than
one hundred shareholders proved to be a protracted and suspenseful
affair. There were endless complications. Some individuals had lost
their shares, and Hynson had to reissue new ones. Trust departments of
banks had to get the necessary approval of trustees or beneficiaries. The
Coca Cola Bottling Company at Laurel was in possession of some two
hundred shares which it was unable to locate until somebody belatedly
remembered a safety deposit box that had not been opened since the
1930s. Most stockholders were happy to sell. An individual owning,
say, twenty-five shares of stock that he had long ago written off as
worthless was now faced with the pleasant prospect of receiving more
than $43,000 for them. But some people were not enthusiastic. One
California shareholder informed Hynson that she didn't wish to sell her
five shares—equaling 20 acres—because her economic advisor had told
her that timberland was a valuable investment. In response, Hynson
successfully argued that if *he* lived in California, he would take the
money and buy a piece of land he could look at occasionally, instead of
continuing to own a theoretical 20 acres spread throughout a 42,500-
acre swamp in southeastern Mississippi. Among Mississippi shareholders, there was a considerable amount of peer pressure; people
would call up Morine to find out whether certain other individuals had
sold their stock before making up their minds to sell their own. In all,
hundreds of phone calls and wires went back and forth between
shareholders or trustees and Morine and/or Hynson, until the latter
two were "blue in the face" from explaining the proposed sale again and
again.

On Monday mornings, Morine would call the First National Bank of
Jackson, the depository of tendered shares, to see how many had come
in the previous week. He kept a chart in his office—"it was like the
United Fund"—on which he could record the narrowing gap between

stock already purchased and the shares needed to complete the sale. "It was exciting but draining," says Morine. "Two and a half months can be a long time, and those shares didn't come in fast. Avery Wood, Quisenberry, Hynson, were calling all the time. Just one guy with 150 shares, or two or three minority stockholders acting together, could have screwed the whole deal. All along, we were afraid we might have to go into separate negotiations." Slowly at first, then more rapidly, the gap narrowed. But it was not closed until the day of the deadline, May 14. Ironically, the last shares to be tendered were the Wisners', which came in by the midnight mail on the final day. In the end, everyone had agreed to sell; the Conservancy did not even have to avail itself of the narrow margin that Gardiner Green had provided. "By tendering their stock," says Morine, "the shareholders had committed themselves to make one of the biggest donations to conservation in the nation's history. They gave close to $3.4 million to the Conservancy, and it was that unprecedented sum that made the whole deal possible."

Almost everyone concerned with the long effort to buy and sell the Pascagoula now began to regard the outcome as a certainty. The great swamp would become the property of the state of Mississippi, Avery Wood would have done the "something big" he had dreamed of doing, and Dave Morine would have broken new ground both in conservation's land acquisition policies and the concept of state-run heritage programs. The long struggle had left Morine too numb to be more than moderately pleased, but he did suppose that he could now relax. What remained was mostly lawyer work—arranging for a bank to loan the Conservancy the money to buy Pascagoula Hardwood just long enough to dissolve the company, then sell the land to the state, and pay the bank off. As for the IRS, Healy and Knight both seemed to feel that the agency would have to come through with a favorable ruling; it was not for Morine to manufacture imaginary problems when he had already overcome so many real ones.

This easy attitude of wait-and-see vanished on June 15 when James Knight called Morine to say that he might withdraw his request for a ruling because it would probably be unfavorable when it came. It was customary in these matters for the IRS to advise petitioners in advance of what its ruling would be, thereby giving those concerned an opportunity to withdraw their request in the event that the advance notice was not in their favor. Often in such cases, the parties who had requested the ruling would go ahead with the transaction anyway if they were certain they had a good case, even though they might subsequently have to argue that case in court. However, Knight warned Morine that in this instance, although he felt that he could win in court, there would be no such remedy; Gardiner Green would not go ahead with the sale if there were even a remote chance that he might have to pay taxes as a result of the company's dissolution.

Knight was furious with the IRS, and pessimistic about the outcome of the deal. Morine, however, refused once again to realize that he was beaten. There was nothing he could do directly to appeal the government's advance decision: Knight had already exhausted the recourse of an informal hearing. But if the Internal Revenue Service had no time to spare for him, yet it might not be so indifferent to a request from another branch of the federal government. Morine, operating on sheer gall, called the office of the assistant secretary of the interior, Nathaniel Reed. Reed had been helpful to the Conservancy on more than one occasion, and Morine figured that it couldn't hurt to try him again. Reed was on vacation in the Rockies, but his office promised to let him know that Morine was urgently trying to reach him. Reed returned the call and after learning what had happened, agreed to an unusual move. He gave Morine the name of one of the higher-ups at IRS whom he should contact. Reed himself advised this same official that the Pascagoula project was of national significance. After some haggling, Morine was granted an additional hearing at which he could present his case. However, Reed warned Morine that it would be up to him and his lawyers to turn the IRS around.

The meeting was set up for August 3, 1976. Morine was now more desperately worried about the project than he had ever been. Time was running out; the terms of the tender offer had to be met by August 10, less than a week away. The state could not advertise the sale of bonds, ordinarily a fairly drawnout procedure, until the IRS ruling was obtained. And until the bonds were sold, the state, of course, could not buy the property. As had been the case with Masonite, it seemed possible that a federal ruling might again prevent the sale of the Pascagoula Hardwood Company.

On the appointed day, Morine, Knight, Healy, and the Conservancy's two New York tax attorneys, Stanley Weithorn and Ray Rubin, gathered in a subterranean room in the vast federal maze on Constitution Avenue. There they were met by four IRS men. Two of these were the lawyers with whom Knight had already had a row about the decision; a third man was evidently their supervisor, and the fourth was an official of high rank in the IRS hierarchy. According to Morine, "it was obvious that the two younger guys were uncomfortable. All they wanted to do was put their time in, get out, and make some money as tax lawyers. If this hearing went against them it would be a stain on their records. In addition, they may have been intimidated by Stanley Weithorn. He'd practically written the federal tax code on charitable giving. So they had to prove they were right. Their immediate supervisor was upset too; he'd look like hell if they'd made a mistake. The only guy who seemed open-minded was the big honcho. Of course, lawyers can't agree on anything, so it was one hostile meeting; nobody liked anybody. There were ten people and I was the only nonlawyer. I'd been told not to say a word. Right away they start going at each other, no courtesy; they were throwing sections of the tax code at each other like spears. It was a circus!"

The argument raged back and forth for more than an hour. The IRS lawyers insisted that the Nature Conservancy and Pascagoula Hardwood had entered into an informal agreement on a method of liquidating the company without filing an advance notice, thereby breaking a regulation in the code. Knight and the Conservancy lawyers countered that this view was absurd because many conditions in the tender offer had not as yet been met. Morine, watching from the sidelines, remembered an earlier occasion when he had also been an outsider whom no one had especially wanted to listen to at first. On that occasion—

Senator Bodron's Appropriations Committee meeting—he had railed about the loss of Mississippi's way of life. "That time, it was the Pascagoula that had prevailed against inertia and the committee rules. I figured that maybe I could pull the same stunt again. So to everybody's horror, I stood up and said: 'What the hell is going on? Here's the finest natural area in the land, and unless you people resolve your disagreements, we're going to lose it for future generations!' Well, they all looked at me like I had leprosy or something. These guys couldn't have cared less about a mere swamp. I was an idiot; with important things like interpretation of tax codes at stake, who the hell cared about what happened to 32,000 acres of the finest bottomland left in America."

With Morine squelched, the debate continued. Eventually a compromise was worked out between the lawyers. The IRS attorneys agreed that if the request for a ruling were reworded, they could act favorably on it. The substance would not be changed, but apparently an alteration in the verbiage would disassociate this case from some other more important and somewhat similar one in which the IRS intended to come to a negative conclusion; so, at least, the amazed Weithorn and Rubin theorized.

Morine was relieved, but the time problem remained. In order to remain on schedule, the whole matter would have to be cleared up within three days. Knight had the amended request ready within twenty-four hours, and Morine hand delivered it to the IRS the next day. The two "underlings" who had hexed the ruling from the first were now in no great hurry to set matters right. One day was lost because their typist was "unavailable," and another because one of them left the office early. "They were little people," Morine observes with rare bitterness. "But finally, on the third day, we got the necessary approval and Knight flew down to Mississippi with it that evening. We were cutting it close, but it was beginning to look like we'd make it. Just before I left for Jackson, Pat Noonan called to see how things were going. He and his family were at Disneyland on vacation. I told him, 'Don't expect to see Mickey Mouse down there; he's working for the IRS.' "

During the next few weeks, life was hectic for the participants in the

Pascagoula sale, but the transaction proceeded on schedule. Two Jackson banks, Deposit Guaranty and the First National, loaned the Nature Conservancy the $13.5 million necessary to purchase stock, the largest private loan ever made in the history of conservation. Dave Morine became the president of Pascagoula Hardwood, from which post he presided over the partitioning of the property with the Green interests and the dissolution of the company during the following week. Thanks to the special efforts of the state bond supervisor, Grover Allen, and an assistant attorney general, Sam Birdsong, the state bonds were readied for sale with exceptional dispatch. On August 24, they were purchased by Chase Manhattan Bank at a favorable interest rate of 4.8997 percent.

There was one final hitch. Morine wanted the deed of transfer to the state to stipulate that the primary purpose of all managment plans for the Pascagoula property would be the preservation of wildlife habitat. In this he was supported by the members of the Heritage Committee. However, Bruce Garretty, acting as the state's attorney in drawing up the deed, insisted upon a deed that would be "clean" of any such restrictions. There was some irony in this situation; three years earlier, Garretty had been the first of Avery Wood's advisors to advocate legislation that would facilitate the acquisition of wildlife habitat in Mississippi. Now, as an attorney acting for the state, he would not yield an inch. "It put a cloud over the proceedings," Morine shrugs. But there was no backing away now. He had to sign. During every moment that the Conservancy continued to hold the property, the interest on more than $13 million was ticking away "like the meter in a taxicab." After affixing his signature, Morine walked out of the room without a word. Avery Wood, who was with him, angrily assailed Garretty in the corridor outside, but to no effect; it was Garretty's turn to walk away. "I was pretty depressed," Morine says. "I knew we had sympathetic government in Mississippi for the moment, but what about later on? It would be too bad if timber interests or even recreational interests won out against ecological values." Then he brightens. "But all things have their positive side. We left realizing that our job wasn't over. We would have to improve the heritage program to protect it from things like this."

By September 22, 1976, when the deed to the Pascagoula tract was ceremoniously transferred from the Nature Conservancy to the Mississippi Wildlife Heritage Committee at an official luncheon, the emphasis was on the positive. Government officials, legislators, former shareholders in Pascagoula Hardwood, bankers, and a contingent from the Conservancy were all on hand. The congratulatory speeches were short, the food was good, and everyone enjoyed the showing of the Pascagoula film. While the audience watched the pageant of the swamp unfold, Morine, Quisenberry, and Wood watched the smiling audience. Morine was thinking about the distance some of these people had traveled during the last three years towards the realization of a conservation ethic, and wondering where they would go from here. Quisenberry was recalling a conversation he had had with Bob Hynson prior to the luncheon, during which he had asked what odds Hynson would have given two years earlier against this scene ever taking place. The former president of Pascagoula Hardwood had replied that back then "I hadn't reckoned on the sheer tenacity of people like you and Dave Morine."

As for Avery Wood, he had done the one important thing he had wanted to do; but he knew that in a few more days he would no longer be director of the Mississippi Game and Fish Commission. He was wondering what he would do with the rest of his life.

CHAPTER XII

The Future

THE PRESERVATION of the Pascagoula was a "first" in several respects. It was the largest tract ever acquired by a state out of its own funds for the purpose of wildlife management; it was the largest bottomland overflow swamp ever to receive protection; it was the first major property ever purchased by a conservation organization by means of a complex tender offer; it involved the largest private loan (13.5 million) in the history of conservation.

However, as far as the Nature Conservancy is concerned, the real importance of this transaction lies elsewhere. The Conservancy after all, has been involved in the acquisition of other wild areas of comparable size—among them, the chain of barrier islands along the Virginia coast, the Santee Hunt Club in South Carolina, and, more recently, Santa Cruz Island in California. And, in terms of the strict criteria set down by the Conservancy's scientific director, Bob Jenkins, many other tracts have been rescued that could outclass even the Pascagoula in terms of their ecological worth, places such as Hungry Beech in West Virginia with its virgin cove forest and rare ferns; or South Carolina's Stevens Creek which harbors zig-zag salamanders and a shrub, *Rebes echivellum*, so rare it has no common name; or the Skagit River Sanctuary in Washington which protects the largest wintering concentration of bald eagles in the Pacific Northwest. Even Morine's strategy in effecting a sale, though exceptional of its kind, was not more original or daring than the business strategies devised on occasion by Pat Noonan and other wheeler-dealers at the Conservancy.

In the larger view, which takes in not only the Conservancy's still evolving aims but the entire field of land preservation, the great importance of saving the Pascagoula Swamp lay in the credibility it established for the organization's heritage programs. It is in this respect that the "firsts" count most: although Georgia and South Carolina had paved the way, this was the first time the Conservancy had worked with state legislators and agency heads to develop a truly comprehensive plan to preserve a state's most vulnerable and unique natural resources. That program included: (1) the creation of a relatively independent state agency designed to identify, protect, and manage that state's threatened resources; (2) the implementation of a computerized "element specific" inventory of the state's fauna and flora, and the ecosystems containing them; (3) the practice of preidentifying lands of exceptional ecological worth and then initiating efforts to protect them rather than acquiring wild lands in a haphazard manner as they became available; (4) the methodology for working with state government to finance land acquisition, and with the federal government (through Land and Water Conservation Funds) to finance an ongoing inventory.

The novelty of this approach cannot be sufficiently emphasized. The idea of a private conservation group and a state government working systematically as a team had not been tried before. The idea of a continuing biological inventory and the preidentification of threatened resources on any level, state or federal, had never previously existed. Indeed, on the state level, where the heritage program could be most effectively applied, it was the rule for governmental agencies and professional biologists to be unaware of even the most fundamental facts about their states' ecological assets. Exactly how many acres of, say, brush clover remained in Missouri and where were they to be found? What were the number and locations of wading bird rookeries in Maryland? How many endemic species of minnows and other small fish (or snails, or salamanders, or turtles) were known to exist in West Virginia, and in what obscure creeks and streams did they survive?

Even in the case of highly visible or publicized species, ignorance was the rule. How many active golden eagle aeries in Idaho, and where?

How many virgin stands of cypress in Arkansas or hickory in Connect-
icut, and where? The answers to such questions had previously existed,
if at all, only in fragmented bits and pieces, rarely updated and never
assimilated as part of a computerized data base. In every state, wildlife
agencies were committed almost exclusively to the management of
game species, forestry commissions were concerned only with commercial timber, and parks and recreation departments cared only about
camping and hiking opportunities for their human constituents. If rare
species of flora and fauna were protected at all, it was usually by
accident. The track record at the universities was not—and still isn't—
much better; for every study of the ringtailed cat, the gray owl, the swift
fox, or even the javelina, there were a thousand, many of them redun-
dant, on the white-tailed deer or the cottontail rabbit. Moreover, the
information that was gathered on rare, or rarely studied species, was
often, as Jenkins would say, "doomed to oblivion" because it was soon
outdated and/or because it existed in isolation without reference to any
inventory or habitat acquisition plan that applied to the species in
question. "When we went into one state," Jenkins recalls, "they didn't
even know how many state parks they had, much less what was in
them; they were yelling down the halls, asking if anybody had a list."

In contrast to this general rule of chaos, ignorance, and duplicated
effort, the Mississippi Wildlife Heritage Program was now collecting all
the available data on every vulnerable species and ecosystem known, or
suspected, to be present in the state. This material was fed into a
computer data bank, cross-referenced, and applied, if not for habitat
acquisition, then to fend off development in places where rare species
were to be found. In the case of the Pascagoula, although the swamp
had been "sold" to the public—justifiably—as a public hunting and
fishing area, it was now possible to catalog all the valuable and unusual
life forms it supported, a type of scrutiny to which no other state wildlife
management area had ever been subjected on a comprehensive scale.

If the purchase of the Pascagoula gave credibility to the Mississippi
Heritage Program, that program has now strengthened the Nature
Conservancy's influence in other states. There are presently seventeen

active state heritage programs, plus one with the TVA. By the time this book is published, several others will have begun. All are different. Some states have natural resource agencies that are able to centralize all the activities of the program; in others, the program's activities are parceled out among different and not always friendly bureaucracies. In some states, political considerations are more a factor than in others. But in spite of these variations on the Conservancy's platonic ideal of the perfect heritage program (Mississippi still comes as close to that as any), Jenkins declares that "we aren't ashamed of any of them." In all of them, the triad of heritage goals, inventory (or identification), protection (by acquisition or other means), and stewardship, are in progress, usually with impressive results. Jenkins's greatest concern is for his brainchild, the ecological inventory. He is pleased that in every state heritage program the inventory methodology is the same. What he frets about most is the problem of continuity. "These inventories aren't projects, you know, something you do once and that's it," Jenkins admonishes. "They are an accounting process that keeps track of new discoveries, landscape changes, changes in ecofunction, or in the status of a species, even changes in the science of biological classification. All these things have to be kept up with on an ongoing basis or pretty soon everything falls apart again. That's the problem with almost all government projects. There's so little continuity in federal projects that they pay again to find out what they just learned three years ago. And they don't learn much because they're always at the alpha level. Before they reach beta, the funds are cut off again."

The Nature Conservancy is now trying, for the second time, to have a "Natural Diversity Act" passed in Washington which will ensure national recognition of the heritage program and provide much of its funding on the state level in a direct and dependable way. On the first attempt, the Conservancy was not adequately prepared for the resistance of big business lobbyists who—mistakenly—envisaged the proposed legislation as a new twist on the endangered species act. This time around, the Conservancy planners hope to convince opposition forces that the bill will serve their interests by indicating, before environmental impact statements are required or development gets underway, whether or not their activities will pose environmental problems that might, as in the case of the Tellico Dam, subject them to government regulations or a suit. However, even if the Conservancy makes its point, a budget-conscious Congress will be hard to persuade. Meantime, the Conservancy is moving, on its own, towards a national inventory system. It has contracted with the National Science Foundation to collect information on "established scientific ecological reserves" into a single computer data base. It is also gathering information from its own study of preserved lands and the various state heritage program systems to supplement the NSF project, with the intent of establishing the groundwork for a nationwide data bank system for all important natural areas in the country.

Jenkins hopes that the heritage program will set into action a process he calls "entrainment," a syndrome in which more and more groups and individuals—including the federal government, become dependent on the data provided by the heritage programs. As the programs become indispensable, their continuity will be assured. Already, every state that has initiated the program has received anywhere from dozens to hundreds of requests from governmental entities like highway departments, the Soil Conservation Service, the Corps of Engineers and such private interests as utility companies, gas and oil corporations, timber interests —all wanting to know before they start damming, digging, or cutting, whether they will run into some trouble-making snail darter, lousewort, or nesting sandhill crane. Even more promising, in terms of Jenkins's entrainment theory, some of these agencies and corporations are providing funds for the inventories. The federal government already contributes substantially through Land and Water Conservation Funds (which must, however, be assigned by the states). In Indiana, the nonfederal share is paid for by public utility companies; in New Mexico, the original backing came from oil interests; in a couple of other states timber companies contribute.

But if the inventory is doing well, the Conservancy still has its work cut out for it when it comes to acquisition and other methods of protection. In a memorandum to department heads concerning the Conservancy's 1985 goals, Greg Low, the organization's business manager, reports: "Despite our overall progress, a look outside the Conservancy shows an enormous job that remains to be done. The need to preserve natural diversity is imperative. Inventories in Ohio, Indiana, Illinois, North Carolina, Tennessee, Mississippi, Oregon and other states have each cited over 150 highly significant natural areas which should be protected to preserve their respective state's natural diversity. . . . It has been estimated that 15 percent of the remaining types of plant and animal species in the U.S. will disappear within the next twenty years unless action is taken to preserve their habitats. . . . We must face some hard choices—both as a society and a conservation organization—as to which remaining lands are most in need of protection. Since growth cannot be stopped, we should seek to channel growth away from the relatively small portions of the landscape that we can least afford to lose. We must carefully set out to identify and preserve high quality examples of each kind of biological element, or many of them will inevitably be overlooked and unnecessarily destroyed. The need to preserve natural diversity is the most critical of all land use issues and deserves our highest priority. Only in this area are our failures irrevocable." Inevitably, the Conservancy's policy of becoming more and more selective complicates the deal-making process. But it isn't only that: "The resource base is shrinking," says Dave Morine. "There just aren't the great tracts available that there used to be. People used to come to us with news of some terrific swamp or prairie that needed saving. Now there are no big surprises like the Pascagoula anymore. We know about most of what's left. And the competition gets rougher all the time. We're going to have to get away from black and white areas and get into a lot of gray ones. In Mississippi, for example, we've made it possible for people to register their land or dedicate it if it's ecologically interesting. They get a tax exemption and retain the land; and the state gets an option to buy if and when it's for sale."

The Conservancy has learned to arrange many other "gray" solutions involving easements and landowners' good will. In a typical case, a Conservancy volunteer spots an active eagle nest in a tract owned by a large timber company. The Conservancy's regional or state representative confirms the find, contacts the company (with which the Conservancy, often as not, has already established cordial relations) and an eagle expert is called in; recommendations are made, and the timber company agrees not to disturb a tract of forest near the nest. In another scenario, the Conservancy decides to leave a small but ecologically notable bog to its own devices because it has no potential for commercial exploitation.

However, acquisition is still the major aim. The Conservancy's president, Pat Noonan, confirms Morine's view that the larger pieces of land, the "sexy deals," are getting hard to come by. He regards the estate tax law as one of the chief problems: "It forces beneficiaries to pay whopping estate taxes and the only alternative they have is to sell the estate itself. And only the developers and entrepreneurs can pay the price. I predict that our future Pascagoulas are going to be put together like jigsaw puzzles, making twenty or thirty deals for separate tracts instead of one big deal. We have a tremendous task ahead." Noonan seems not at all daunted by this thought. "We've already begun concentrating on ecological quality, not quantity, and from now on we'll be doing a lot more of that." To emphasize this, he recites the Nature Conservancy's latest motto: "The last of the least, the best of the rest."

As for the management of the lands already owned by the Conservancy, the quality of stewardship on these preserves is "at an all-time high," according to the organization's 1982 program report written by business manager Greg Low. At least 90 percent of the preserves are "adequately managed," largely by unpaid volunteers among Conservancy members. However, the threatened loss of real estate tax exemptions for nonprofit organizations is a potential time bomb waiting to explode. According to Low's figures, the loss of the exemption in Westchester County, New York, alone would result in a minimum Conservancy tax liability of $50,000. For this reason, the Conservancy has continued to cut down on the number of preserves retained in its own name, preferring, more than ever, to transfer them to appropriate government agencies. It is also trying, with some success, to transfer out a number of its previously acquired preserves that are of limited ecological significance. On the other hand, the hundreds of thousands of acres that remain in the Conservancy's hands are being used more than ever to conduct inventories and other scientific studies, to educate local people to the importance of natural diversity, and to serve as models of how rare species and habitats should be preserved and protected.

To a considerable degree, the problems and challenges that confront the Conservancy are the byproducts of its own success. Indeed, the managerial staff seems more alarmed than smug about its accomplishments. The energy that still pervades the Arlington headquarters is now less that of a commando unit than a command post during a major battle that is far from won. Strategies, statistics, five-year plans abound; the future imperfect is everyone's favorite subject: Where is the nation heading? the environmental movement? the Conservancy? For these driving and driven people, the future is both a challenge and a threat.

"How do we not peak out?" Greg Low asks rhetorically. He has the answer ready: "As long as we concentrate on saving ecological diversity —we're the only ones doing that—we don't need to worry. Areas don't have to be pristine or huge to be important, as long as they protect the rare whippity-whip or whatever. Look at Bluff Mountain in North Carolina—just a few hundred acres—we had to buy it ourselves—but it protects a whole bunch of rare and endangered species: My God, we're as excited about that as any of our bigger holdings.

"The irony that I find," he goes on, "is that as the Conservancy becomes well-established and prospering, and as we decentralize our efforts—you know, moving into the states with our heritage programs and so on—all the excitement and fun is at the state level instead of here. We're going to have thirty state offices by 1980, and all our top quality people want to stay in their states—they don't want to come to the central office to be managers. Salary doesn't count that much. A typical state has more than one hundred areas of varying size that need to be

protected. Figure we get five of them a year, which is damn good. That
means we got a long way to go before we peak out."

Morine, on the other hand, enjoys referring to himself as a dinosaur.
"I'm obsolete," he declares cheerfully. "When I started in '71, we had 50
people, we put deals together, we were the pioneers. Now we have 250
employees, we have a bunch of scientists, we have a legislative arm.
Everything is more complex." Morine believes that in the South, for a
few more years at least, it will still be possible to make the sort of deals
he likes to make. "It's not that way out West," he says. "Take for
example the Platte River in Nebraska. The U.S. Fish and Wildlife
Service asked us to help them preserve a long stretch of the Platte that is
habitat for the largest concentration of sandhill cranes in all of North
America. We soon found out that we could buy all the land along this
stretch of the river and it wouldn't do a damn bit of good. The whole
issue revolves around water rights. To preserve the habitat you have to
guarantee a minimum flowage. So the question becomes who has the
most rights to the water—farmers, utility companies, towns and munic-
ipalities, industry, or finally, the wildlife that have been using the Platte
since day one. It's a nightmare, but it's also the first major example of
how we as a country are going to allocate finite resources." The only
people who are sure to win, in Morine's view, are the lawyers. "They'll
be litigating over who has rights to what from now until doomsday. If
the Conservancy wants to get involved in these kinds of issues, and I
imagine that we will, we are going to have to recruit a different type of
staff. In fact we will become a different type of organization."

Morine feels that the Southeast still has ten more years before the
"nightmare" catches up with it. "That's why we are formulating a plan
to protect a million acres of southern streams, swamps, and bottomland
hardwoods before 1990. Through our heritage programs, we are going
to involve industry, government, and concerned individuals. All the
pieces are there; all we have to do is to put them together, before growth
and the mumbo-jumbo lawyers track us down."

In spite of Morine's conviction that he is becoming obsolete, he continues his usual frenetic and passionate pursuit of deals. He is on San Pedro River one day, working out an acquisition strategy with the Conservancy's western regional office; and on the Snake the next, reviewing a plan to acquire key inholdings in the area that the Bureau of Land Management has designated as a raptor sanctuary. In spite of the Conservancy's talk about smaller but more select parcels of land, Morine still has a fondness for the really big projects, the "impossible" deals. His current obsession is a 50,000-acre tract of bottomland forest in northwestern Louisiana, part of a 125,000-acre holding known as the Chicago Mills Lumber Company. The entire area will be cleared for soybeans if the deal he is negotiating between the owners and the federal government falls through.

Chicago Mills is an interesting example of the Conservancy's evolving view that an area's ecological importance is not necessarily tied to its "pristine" quality. The forest in question is heavily managed, with large acreages planted to even-stand trees, others already cleared, and all of it criss-crossed by brutally channelized streams. It could not qualify as any kind of park or wilderness area. Nevertheless it is important in the ecological scheme of things simply because it is the only extensive tract of hardwood forest—any kind of hardwood forest—that remains in northern Louisiana. Morine is convinced that the whirlwind destruction of 23 million acres of bottomlands in the central South—that same unnatural process that made a conservationist of Avery Wood—may well rank as the most ruinous and inexcusable environmental disaster to afflict this nation in the last two decades. The ditch-and-drain projects of the U.S. Corps of Engineers, and the increasing profits to be made from soybeans, have stripped the southern lowlands of one of the planet's most productive ecosystems almost before anyone knew what was going on.

Thus, Chicago Mills achieves its ecological importance by default. It is crowded with deer, turkeys, wildcats, perhaps a few panthers, and a large percentage of the few black bears surviving in the south central states. Like India's Gir Forest, it is a sort of housing project for an indigenous fauna that literally has no place else to go. "The Pascagoula, it's not," grouses Morine. "And the price! Holy mackerel! But it's all that's left, and the black bears are still there; I've seen their tracks myself. So we've *got* to save it."

Pat Noonan takes a more administrative view of the Conservancy's prospects. "The conservation movement is going to get caught in a boomerang effect before long. The seventies saw a lot of environmental regulation, but we may have gone too far. People are tolerant when they're fat and happy; but when they're waiting in line at the gas station it's a different story. There's going to be a lot more compromise in the eighties; and the environmentalists are going to have to be more coordinated if they're going to get their share. We're the least regulated industry in this country; we've got to come together more. Myself, I see the Conservancy at the prow of the ship in the conservation movement. The heritage programs are going to be responsible for that; everyone's going to turn to them. Of course," he adds, with an into-the-breach set of the jaw, "some programs will falter, some will fail; but the majority will go forward." He is already thinking ahead to the year 2000. He hints at the idea of trust funds and revolving accounts that will keep the inflationary wolf from the Conservancy's door. He even speaks cautiously of going international: "A tough decision; we already have one man on that—but how much of our limited resources can we invest? I want to go slow, maybe two or three projects in a couple of countries. I'm not sure I like the odds right now. Still, if the early returns are good. . . ." Nothing, after all, is impossible.

In Mississippi, Bill Quisenberry now occupies an office a few steps away from the one in which Avery Wood once stared at his now vanished blackboard. As Wood had hoped, Quisenberry has survived political transitions and continues as the efficient, unassuming director of the state's heritage program. A full-time team of biologists under the direction of a young scientist, Joe Jacob, continues to add to a now formidable inventory of the state's ecological resources, pinpointing the location and status of dozens of floral and faunal species that Mississippi had not even known it possessed. The relationship with the Conservancy is as close as ever and Morine is a frequent and welcome visitor. With his help, a particularly valuable 808-acre expanse of Delta bottomlands known as the McIntyre Scatters has been added to an existing wildlife management area in Leflore County. In Wilkinson County, Clark Creek, a 1,000-acre tract, containing a series of majestic waterfalls—a rarity in Mississippi—has been acquired, part of it donated by International Paper as a charitable deduction, the rest purchased by federal matching funds at no cost to the state. But Mississippi continues to provide funds when they are needed. With $2.5 million appropriated by the legislature, Morine has closed a deal that adds 3,000 additional acres to the Pascagoula Management Area. In addition to these acquisitions, Conservancy-sponsored legislation has also been enacted which makes it possible for owners of ecologically valuable lands to receive tax exemptions by dedicating their property to be managed and protected by the state. For much of this political support, Quisenberry and Morine can thank their long-time legislative allies, notably Don Strider and Charles Deaton.

In New York, Washington, and Laurel, the various members of the Four Families go about the serious business of being quietly successful. Bob Hynson and Gardiner Green still occupy their offices in the imposing family headquarters at Laurel, with no thought of retiring. Green complains mildly that the divisioning of the Pascagoula property, in spite of the hard-line bargaining of his agent, Vardaman, does not wholly satisfy him; and in Washington, Ellis Wisner wonders whether the people of Mississippi are sufficiently aware that his family's decision to sell was largely motivated by public spiritedness. Both he and Hynson also feel that the integrity of the Pascagoula wilderness is still not adequately protected by the state, and point to the recent ceding of a small piece of the tract to a Waterway Authority as evidence for their concern. But in general the clan is satisfied with the way things have turned out. Most of them take genuine pleasure in the knowledge that, management problems notwithstanding, their legacy will enrich the lives of countless people for generations to come. On a more practical level, they have only to note the current value of Masonite shares—for which they had once been prepared to exchange the swamp —to be reminded that Morine's deal was a profitable one.

As for Avery Wood, he sees himself, accurately and without self-pity, as odd man out. He has gone back to work for the Greenwood firm that employed him before he became director of the Game and Fish Commission; most of his spare time he devotes to his two children. The four years in Jackson exist in his memory as an interlude separate from the overall context of his life. His previous experiences had not automatically led him to that high point; and the years that followed have not really seemed to follow. "Sure, I miss all that," he says. "How could I help but miss it?" Yet, at times, it almost seems as though "all that" had happened to someone else.

If Wood is odd man out, Graham Wisner is odd man in. Wisner, who was not sure what he wanted to do with his life, eventually decided that he liked what Morine was doing with his. But when he applied for a job at the Conservancy he was turned down. Twice. It just didn't seem likely that the restless young man who had scandalized Morine on the trip to Jackson would fit in very well with the Nature Conservancy's overwhelmingly businesslike image. In time, however, Graham's persistence reminded Morine that Wayne Jackson, the now deceased Washington attorney whose luncheon meeting with the young man had set the Pascagoula deal into motion, and whose opinion Morine respected, had once remarked that Graham would do well at anything he believed in. The third time Wisner applied, Morine hired him. Jackson's prophecy has proved correct. After a one-year apprenticeship in the Northwest, Wisner now is working directly for Morine and has assumed responsibility for the Conservancy's programs in Alabama, Mississippi, Louisiana, and Arkansas.

Comtemplating this development, Morine, at age 35, is again briefly assaulted by the dinosaur mood: "The Conservancy is racing along; we now have a program that will preserve biological diversity in the United States, maybe the whole world. You have to wonder when people like

Noonan, Low, Jenkins, and myself are going to have to pass the baton to others. I have no desire to get into international situations. Graham does. The world is a smaller place to people like him. When I went to Mississippi I was going to a foreign country. You're not going to find me in the Amazon. Whereas Graham takes that kind of thing for granted. . . . Nowadays we're buying corporations like Pascagoula Hardwood all the time. But there are all sorts of new deals, new approaches requiring new people, that will be just as original in their time as the Pascagoula deal was. There's a whole new wave that will build on that base." He laughs shortly. "Graham always understood that. He always had my number; I just didn't have his."

Then he tells his secretary to put in a call to someone in Louisiana. There are those black bears at Chicago Mills, maybe even a panther or two, that have got to be saved.

INDEX

Allen, Bill, 72, 81, 112, 126
Amherst, 53
Anderson, Polly, 110
Antioch College, 5, 7, 13
Audubon Society, 13, 32
Barrett, Bill, 18, 20, 23, 25, 69
Birdsong, Sam, 162
Bodron, Sen. Ellis, 120-23, 125-27
Brady, Bruce, 72-73
Brandon Company, 133-34
Brown, Mrs. W. Lyon, 147
Burgin, Sen. Bill, 119-20, 124-27
Cannon, Bud, 146, 150
Carraway, T. J., 146
Carter, Jimmy, 41
Central Oil Company, 7, 11, 130, 133, 143
Chisholm, Alexander Field, 130, 133, 143
Chisholm, Elizabeth, 7
Coca Cola Bottling Co., 157
Committee for the Preservation of Natural
   Conditions, 32
Conservancy, 13-14; defined, 28; objectives, 30;
   33, 35-36; techniques for acquiring land, 57;
   66; 86-87, 96, 110-11, 118, 123-24, 131, 135,
   142, 146, 149, 153, 155, 160, 162-63;
   influence of, 164-65
Deaton, Rep. Charles, 68-69, 71-72, 80, 111-18;
   127, 141, 154-55, 175
De Grummond, Mickey, 64-65
Department of Wildlife and Marine
   Resources 46
Ducks Unlimited, 23
Ecological Society of America, 32
Ecologists Union, 33
Finch, Cliff, 155
Gaddis, Billy, 117
Gardiner, George S., 83, 130
Garretty, Bruce, 15, 27, 58, 162

Georgia Heritage Trust, 41
Gibbs, Denton, 85
Gollott, Rep. Tommy, 72
Grassy Lake, 74-75, 80
Green, Eleanor, 147-48
Green, Gardiner, 12, 84-87, 130, 133, 142-44,
   146-47, 149, 150-54, 156, 158-59, 175
Havens, Rep. Lynn, 72
Holland, Bill, 28
Healy, Tom, 148-49, 150, 162-63, 158, 160
House Appropriations Committee, 58, 113,
   119
Humpke, John, 60
Hurricane Camille, 22
Hynson, Bob, 11-13, 64, 77, 81, 83-84, 86-87,
   110, 118-19, 129-32, 142-48, 150, 156-58, 163,
   175
International Paper Company, 80-81, 86, 117,
   118
Jackson, Wayne, 3-6, 13-14, 30, 32, 131, 176
Jacob, Joe, 174
Jenkins, Bob, 36, 40, 42, 43-46, 66, 164-65
Jones, Rick, 60
Kingman, Ed, 34
Kissinger, Henry, 13
Knight, James P., 150-53, 158, 160-61
Lindsay, Jean Gardiner Chisholm, 133-35,
   138, 144-45
Low, Greg, 35-36, 38, 169-70; quoted, 171-72
Mann, Jack, 146
Martin, Willie, 23
Masonite Corporation, 13, 30-31, 63-64, 75, 81,
   84-85, 89, 112, 118
May, William, 147
Mengel Corporation, 84
Mississippi Bureau of Outdoor Recreation, 56,
   60, 65-66, 95
Mississippi Game and Fish Commission, 15,

16-17, 23, 25, 28, 50, 56, 60, 64, 74, 79, 103, 111, 119, 120
Mississippi Heritage Committee, 145
Mississippi Flyway Council, 28
Mississippi State Forestry Commission, 117, 127, 139-40
"Mississippi-the-way-it-is," 23, 25-26
Mississippi Wildlife Federation, 110
Mississippi Wildlife Heritage Committee, conception, 59; 65, 73-75, 79-81, 85, 102, 105, 109-11, 120, 140, 142; new members in 1976, 155-56; accepts Pascagoula tract, 163; 166
Montgomery, Sen. Ray, 71
Morine, Dave: vice-president of Conservancy, 28-29; 31, 29, ecological theory, 40; 47, 51, 63, 70, 72-76, 78-87, 102-07, 110-16; 120-24, 128, 131-34, 136-42, 144-47, 150-64; quoted, 169, 172, 175, 176-77
Murrah, Herman, 9-11, 89-101
National Science Foundation, 168
Natural Heritage Program, 60
Natural Heritage Trust, 59
Nature Conservancy, see "Conservancy"
Nature Conservancy News, 39
Neal, Rep. "Farmer" Jim, 72
Noonon, Pat: nature conservancy president, 29, 33-34, 37, 40, 137-40; 147-48, 161, 164, 170; quoted, 174
Pascagoula Hardwood Company, 8-9, 11-13, 30, 63, 75, 80-81, 83-85, 89, 102, 110-12, 116-19, 123, 129-33, 135-36, 139, 142-43, 148, 153, 160, 163
Pascagoula River, 8, 83, 92
Pascagoula Swamp, 7, 9, 30, 64, 76, 88, 105, 109, 122, 127
Pearl River Basin, 64, 112
Quisenberry, Bill, 15, 20, 27-28, 63, 65, 71, 78-83, 85-86, 88-101, 102-111, 116-119, 122-124, 126-27, 129, 132, 141-42, 145, 146, 154-55, 158, 163, 174
Reed, Nathaniel, 159

Rhodes, Sen. "Son," 71, 120
Rubin, Ray, 160-61
Saint-Amand, Cynthia, 134
Sanders, Rae, 61, 66, 68, 95, 96
Securities and Exchange Commission, 31, 64, 75
Senate Game and Fish Committee, 59, 74, 120
Sierra Club, 32
Smith, Sanford J., 81
Smith, Sen. Martin, 121
Soil Conservation Service, 21
South Carolina Heritage Program, 46
Statewide Comprehensive Outdoor Recreation Plan (SCORP), 61
Strider, Don, 71, 74-75, 80, 113, 119, 120, 125, 127, 141, 155, 175
Thigpen, Bud, 116
Tingle, Melvin, 80, 105, 107
Turner, Ed, 146
U.S. Corps of Engineers, 21
U.S. Dept. of the Interior, 60
Union Camp Corporation, 46
United Fruit Corporation, 5
Vance, Cy, 62
Vardaman, James M., 154, 175
Vaught, John, 72, 112
Waller, Bill, 16-17, 26, 65-67, 69, 72, 78-79, 81, 86, 119, 126, 137, 155
Weithorn, Stanley, 160
Winter, William, 120
Wisner, Ellis, 117-118, 138, 139, 143, 145, 175
Wisner, Frank, Jr., 138
Wisner, Frank, Sr., 5-6
Wisner, Graham, 3-4, 30, 75, 76-77, 79-80, 83-84, 89-90, 92-94, 97-100, 107, 117, 136, 138, 176
Wood, Avery, 15-17, 22, 25, 49, 51, 58-59, 67, 69-72, 74-80, 90, 102-07, 110-28; 129; 140-41, 146, 154-55, 158, 162-63, 173, 176
Wright, Sam, 155

The Mississippi Wildlife Heritage Committee recognizes the pivotal role of the State Legislature in anticipating the need for conservation legislation setting aside land in public ownership for future outdoor recreational opportunities. The farsighted leadership of the many members of the House and Senate who helped create the Committee and encouraged the eventual purchase of the Pascagoula Hardwood tract will be an indelible part of Mississippi's history.

The Committee would be remiss in neglecting the crucial assistance of the many thousands of individuals, sportsman's associations, hunting and fishing clubs, other public and private conservation organizations, civic, religious and social groups that wrote letters and telegrams and made personal contact with members of the Legislature supporting the now nationally recognized Pascagoula Project.

Finally, any mention of this project would be incomplete without recognizing the decisive expertise of The Nature Conservancy. Its board of governors and staff provided the technical, legal and financial guidance related to land acquisition that made this purchase a reality for the people of Mississippi.

The following persons served as members of The Mississippi Wildlife Heritage Committee from its creation on March 11, 1974, through the purchase of the Pascagoula Hardwood Tract on September 22, 1976. The project was initiated during the administration of Governor William Waller and consummated during the administration of Governor Cliff Finch.

Charter Members

William H. Allen	James H. Neal
Bruce H. Brady	William C. Rhodes
Charles M. Deaton	Donald B. Strider
Tommy A. Gollott	John H. Vaught
Ray H. Montgomery	Avery Wood, Jr.

Other Members

Francis S. Bowling	Donald W. Cumbest
Robert H. Burress, Jr.	Nathaniel H. Lewis
Billy Joe Cross	Joe E. Stone
Donald M. Cross	Sam W. Wright